ERASMUS

STUDIES IN LATIN LITERATURE AND ITS INFLUENCE

Editors
D. R. Dudley and T. A. Dorey

CICERO

Chapters by J. P. V. D. Balsdon, M. L. Clarke, T. A. Dorey, A. E. Douglas, R. G. M. Nisbet, H. H. Scullard, G. B. Townend

LUCRETIUS

Chapters by D. R. Dudley, B. Farrington, O. E. Lowenstein, W. S. Maguinness, T. J. B. Spencer, G. B. Townend, D. E. W. Wormell

ROMAN DRAMA

Chapters by W. R. Chalmers, C. D. N. Costa, G. L. Evans, J. A. Hanson, A. Steegman, T. B. L. Webster, T. L. Zinn

LATIN HISTORIANS

Chapters by E. Badian, F. W. Walbank, T. A. Dorey, G. M. Paul, P. G. Walsh, E. A. Thompson, J. Campbell

LATIN BIOGRAPHY

Chapters by Edna Jenkinson, E. L. McQueen, A. J. Gossage, G. B. Townend, A. R. Birley, T. A. Dorey, D. H. Farmer, Rosalind Brooke

VIRGIL

Chapters by M. Ayrton, Brooks Otis, A. J. Gossage, J. H. Whitfield, W. F. J. Knight, R. D. Williams, A. G. MacKay, D. E. W. Wormell

TACITUS

Chapters by T. A. Dorey, C. D. N. Costa, A. R. Burn, K. Wellesley, Norma P. Miller, R. H. Martin, P. Burke

ERASMUS

Chapters by
Margaret Mann Phillips   A. E. Douglas
J. W. Binns   B. Hall
D. F. S. Thomson   T. A. Dorey

Edited by
T. A. DOREY

ROUTLEDGE & KEGAN PAUL
London

First published 1970
by Routledge & Kegan Paul Ltd
Broadway House, 68–74 Carter Lane
London, E.C.4
Printed in Great Britain by
Western Printing Services Ltd, Bristol
© T. A. Dorey, 1970
ISBN 0 7100 6805 0

To the memory of
P. J. Enk

Contents

Introduction

THE year 1969 marked the fifth centenary of the most probable birth-date of Erasmus. The actual year is uncertain, as during the course of his life he found it advisable to advance the date of his birth in order to offer a plausible defence to the charge—probably true—of his enemies that he had been born after his father had taken Holy Orders. It has been one of the great obstacles to the reputation of Erasmus that, born in unfortunate circumstances, with no family influence or financial resources of his own, he was because of his natural genius destined to play a prominent part in the world in which he lived. This great difference between his humble background and the role that he found himself called to fill made it necessary for him, in his earlier years at any rate, to resort to flatteries and subterfuges in order to obtain the patronage he needed both to give him some slight financial security and to afford him protection against the increasingly bitter attacks of his enemies. It can truthfully be said on his behalf that, where to our eyes the behaviour of Erasmus occasionally puts him in a less than creditable light, the fault usually lies in the social circumstances of his times, which did not always permit openness and frankness of behaviour in those of a lower social station. It was only when he attained a status of independence and a high degree of international esteem that he was able to act in a manner more completely in accord with his own real nature.

Erasmus was not merely in the front rank of teachers and reformers, but he was also a great writer of Latin and an outstanding figure in the history of Latin literature. It is mainly in this regard that he has been thought suitable to be the subject of a volume in this series. In the range of his style, his command of language, the variety of the subjects that he covered, and the very size of his output he can only be compared with Cicero. Like Cicero he achieved a position of such eminence that even within his own lifetime anything he wrote was in demand. It is also important to realize that he came almost at the end of a long series of writers, stretching back into the Dark Ages, who kept Latin alive as a medium of literary composition and without whose efforts the rediscovery of Classical authors in the Renaissance would have borne little fruit.

This volume contains chapters on the importance of Erasmus as an interpreter of the Classics, as a satirist, and as a writer of letters. There is an account of his work as a Biblical scholar and religious reformer, an examination of his linguistic style, and a discussion of the Medieval background and the significance of Erasmus to our own times.

T. A. DOREY

I

Erasmus and the Classics

MARGARET MANN PHILLIPS

'A man born to bring back literature, *ad restituendas literas natus,*' said the contemporaries of Erasmus,[1] and this at least remains undisputed; doctrinal controversies may still rage about the extent of his personal commitment to one cause or the other, but there is no doubt of his eminence as a popularizer of the classics. Throughout his life he remained faithful to the cause of rediscovering and restoring the literature of antiquity, and a large proportion of his huge output consists of editions, translations and annotations of classical authors. Yet here, as in every other aspect of Erasmus, there is a very personal attitude to be observed, a delicate balance between values. Whole-hearted as his admiration was, it was never subservient, and he saw the classics strictly in relation to the needs of the modern world. Earnest in his struggle to abolish corrupt texts and misreadings, he was yet not a solemn scholar; there was an element of the journalist in his make-up which banished pomposity and made him take the reader aside in a very human way. The cause of Good Letters, to him, was the cause of humanity, and his enthusiasm for it was balanced by an indignant incredulity, sometimes by a testy irritation, against those who failed to see what was so obvious in his own eyes. It was crystal-clear to him that the qualities discoverable in the writers of Greece and Rome were precisely those needed to reorientate the thinking of his own time.

It was an important factor in the processes of thought of the sixteenth century that Erasmus as a boy had fallen in love with the classics. This was not altogether an easy thing to do in 1480–90, at least in Holland, though there were rumours of what was happening in Italy: 'For when I was a boy, good letters had begun to put out buds again among the Italians, but since the art of printing was either undiscovered or known only to a few, no books got through to us, and those who taught the most un-literary literature reigned supreme and perfectly undisturbed.'[2] Beyond the narrowness of the medieval school curriculum, there was a shining dream. Long afterwards he wrote:

> The wonderful force and energy of nature is proved to me by what I experienced as a boy. At a time when good learning was banned from schools, when there was a dearth of books and teachers, when there was no honour to be gained as an incentive, when everyone turned the student away from those studies and pushed him towards other things, something happened to me which was not the result of judgment—I was too young for that—but of natural instinct, which carried me away as by inspiration to the service of the Muses. I hated anyone whom I knew to be hostile to humane studies, I loved those who delighted in them; as for any-one who had acquired any reputation in this field, I looked up to him with reverence, almost with worship. Now that I am old, I am not ashamed of this. Not that I condemn the studies of others, even if they don't personally attract me—but I understand how frigid, maimed and blind learning is if the help of the Muses is taken away. It is shameful to see how stupidly some people scorn this, the best part of knowledge, calling anything that belongs to old and civilized literature 'mere poetry'.[3]

Elsewhere he uses the same phrase: 'I was carried away by a mysterious force of nature to the study of good letters.'[4] Yet there were some discoverable sources for this enthusiasm. Erasmus first emerges in his letters as a schoolboy writing to his guardian[5] about his father's books and quoting Ovid. It is true that he wants to hurry on the sale of the volumes, which constitute his patri-mony, but they were not all sold—a Juvenal turns up later in his correspondence. They were apparently manuscripts of classical texts which his father had copied himself and brought back from Italy. This father, scholar turned priest, has not perhaps received his due in considerations about Erasmus' youth. He contributed illegitimacy to Erasmus' sea of troubles, and possibly his son saw little of him; but that Italian journey which his son records in his *Compendium Vitae* must have made a great impression on a young listener.

> He made a living by writing, since as yet there was no printing; he wrote a beautiful hand. After living a gay life for a while, he turned to serious studies; he knew Latin and Greek well, and in

2

law studies too he was more proficient than most. For Rome blossomed with learned men in those days. He went to Guarino's lectures. All the authors he transcribed with his own hand.[6]

Even though plague was to carry away his mother and father when the boy was only thirteen, an Erasmus of thirteen would be well able to find inspiration in such a memory.

The main personal encouragement of his youth was the passing sight of Rudolph Agricola, the brilliant Frisian scholar. The visit of this glamorous individual to his school at Deventer was apparently the great memory of his boyhood. Hegius and Sinthis, exceptions to the rule of unsympathetic schoolmasters, were friends of Agricola and shared in this rapturous memory, or as Erasmus put it later on, they were the intellectual sons and he, through them, the grandson of this Northern scholar who came back from Italy via Deventer trailing clouds of glory and of Greek. Erasmus' veneration for him is immortalized in the adage *Quid cani et balneo*,[7] since he remembered what Rudolph Agricola had said about setting a theologian to teach children: 'as out of place as a dog in the bath'. It summed up his feeling about literary education seen only as a preparation for scholastic theology, or Latin learnt only for the dialectic of the schools.

These were flashes across a dull background. Erasmus recollected later the *horrida barbaries* and the hostility to anything in the way of good literature which surrounded him in his youth.[8] An early ambition to go to Italy faded; there was no money. And soon he found himself an Austin canon in the monastery of Steyn. But there was a good library (it is possible that Erasmus' father's books were there, and this motivated his choice of Steyn) and he set out on a programme of self-education which was to continue all his life.

Early letters give some idea of the books he read, especially the correspondence with Cornelius Gerard of Gouda, an early friend who had shared his dormitory at school, had been to Italy, and had helped to lure him to the monastery by describing it as a haven of the Muses. 'I have my guides whom I follow; you may have others, I shan't quarrel with you for that. Mine are: in poetry Virgil, Horace, Ovid, Juvenal, Statius, Martial, Claudian, Persius, Lucan, Tibullus, Propertius; in prose Cicero, Quintilian, Sallust, Terence.'[9] Even in these early days, Italian humanism had given him Lorenzo Valla, whose notes on literary style (*Elegantiae*)

Erasmus paraphrased. The correspondence with Cornelius illustrates very well the deep revulsion Erasmus felt against the educational aims and methods of his own country in the fifteenth century. His enthusiastic championship of the ancient writers and modern humanism against the 'barbarous guides' of his schooldays, the dull texts of John of Garland, Isidore of Seville and their like, led to his first manifesto, a book begun at nineteen and worked on for years, the *Book against the Barbarians* (*Antibarbarorum Liber*). It grew to four books, after being recast in the form of a Platonic dialogue in a rural setting, but most of it was lost in Italy and only the first volume was ever printed. It was directed against the enemies of the new classical learning (new? said Erasmus, but it is older than all your quiddities and quoddities of scholastic debate) and the central theme was one which is basic to all the subsequent work of Erasmus: that to turn to the beautiful literature of the past was not to turn away from Christianity and Christian values, as the enemies of the classics said, but that all that is great in human thought can be turned to the glory of God.

The widening of the horizon that this entailed is the essential characteristic of the work of Erasmus. The study of the classics was not for him an end in itself, though perhaps in the early days of his revulsion from scholastic theology he had swung towards a more dilettante view of literature. Talks with John Colet at Oxford and deeper study soon altered that. It became clear to him about the turn of the century, well before his visit to Italy in 1506, that his mission was to open the eyes of his generation, to convince them that the classics, far from being pagan, were a magnificent inheritance to be used in the cause of Christ. The early Fathers, especially Jerome, encouraged this point of view which had been obscured for many centuries.

The task was primarily linguistic. It was not necessary to worship God in bad grammar; in a way it was as simple as that. If the richness of the classical heritage were to be recognized, and the service of Christ freed both from narrow devotion and from soulless dialectic, it was necessary to have the tools, a purified Latin and above all, Greek; it was necessary to have the texts, to publish the whole obtainable range of the classical authors and the Fathers of the Church, and the Greek text of the New Testament; it was necessary to go further and apply the standards obtained in various forms that would breathe the spirit of antiquity which was

4

also the spirit of the modern world. The distinction of Erasmus lay in his clear vision of the object in view. It was more than a dedicated scholar who was required here. It had to be someone whose ideals of scholarship were high but his sense of the ultimate aim still higher; a practical idealist who could appreciate the necessity for exactitude but could see beyond it to the knitting together of the best in human experience. Erasmus was in this way the man for the hour.

We are concerned here with one side only of this great effort, the rehabilitation and making available to the general public of the Greek and Latin classics. But it is as well to remember, when assessing Erasmus' work in this respect, that he never thought of his classical authors as an end in themselves, only as a necessary and permanent constituent in the reorientation of men's thought towards true values, whether aesthetic, ethical or religious.

There were several ways open to him. The most obvious was the direct exploration of the resources: editions, translations, advice on study and educational methods. A second way of introducing a wider public to the world of antiquity was a personal invention of his own, the *Adagia*, partly anthology, partly commentary, partly collection of essays. A third way of reaching a still wider circle of readers was by original works like the *Praise of Folly* or the *Colloquies* or the incidental writings that flowed from his pen in answer to specific needs, like the dialogue *Ciceronianus*. By studying these widening circles we shall attempt to come to some conclusions about the nature of Erasmus' influence.

We can see too the type of enemy he had to contend with all his life in defence of the New Learning. First it was the reactionary group faithful to the methods of scholastic theology, who regarded all dealings with pagan literature as dangerous and Greek as particularly heretical. The leaders of this army were the theologians of the universities, in Paris or Louvain for instance, and some of the religious orders (particularly, in Erasmus' view, the Franciscans). But there was danger from the other side too, and in the dialogue *Ciceronianus* (1528) Erasmus launched an attack on the enthusiasts of classical literature who would ban the use of any expression which did not occur in Cicero—thus cutting off classical studies from the modern world. Behind this narrow purism he sensed the trend of Italian neo-pagan ideas. And thirdly, the violence of some of the reformers made them, for him, the worst obstacle in the way of the development he had hoped for, the peaceful triumph of Christian humanism. His own intentions were definite: not to over-exalt the classics, but to draw from them that widening and maturing influence which seemed to him utterly in keeping with Christianity.

II

What do translations, editions and prefaces tell us about Erasmus' own attitude to the classics?

The list of the authors edited or translated by Erasmus is long and varied and includes Aristotle, Cicero, Quintus Curtius, Demosthenes, Euripides, Isocrates, Libanius, Livy, Lucian, Ovid, Plautus, Pliny, Plutarch, Seneca, Suetonius, Terence, Xenophon. To these may be added his favourite schoolbook, the *Distichs* of Cato ('My Catunculus') and the Greek grammar of Gaza which he translated into Latin, and the Greek dictionary of Ceratinus to which he wrote a preface.[10]

There are two points to bear in mind when reading this list. In the first place, it does not necessarily supply us with a complete picture of Erasmus' tastes and preferences, as the task of putting the classics before the public was a joint enterprise between author and publisher, and the great scholar-printers of the Renaissance like Aldus and Froben had no doubt as much to do with the choice of authors as the scholars who edited the texts. In the same way the large range of literature represented in the *Adagia* does not tell us everything about Erasmus' reading, because some literary genres are much more likely to produce proverbial sayings than others. It is for this reason that the dramatists, and particularly Aristophanes, play such a large part in the *Adagia*. Secondly, there was a difference in Erasmus' dealings with his Latin and Greek texts. The list given to Cornelius Gerard in 1489 consisted entirely of Latin authors. It was not until he had managed to get to Paris around 1495 that Erasmus was able to turn seriously to the study of Greek, of which he says he had had only the slightest tincture as a boy. It was in 1500–1501, when he was long past thirty, that he eventually came to grips with it. In March 1500 he writes despondently that the effort to learn Greek is killing him; he has no leisure, and no money to buy books or pay a teacher.[11] In April, 'As soon as I get some money I shall buy

Greek books and then clothes.'[12] In September, regretfully returning a copy of Homer, 'I burn with such love of this author that though I can't understand him, the very sight of the book does me good.'[13] About this time he began to translate Homer, as one of his pupils, Pyrrhus d'Angleberme, remembered.[14] In 1501 he writes: 'I have had the luck to get hold of some Greek things and I spend my days and nights in copying them out on the quiet. Someone may ask why I am so keen on following the example of Cato the Censor as to want to learn Greek at my age. If I had been of this mind as a boy, or rather if the times had been propitious to me, I should have been far happier.' However, he thinks, better late than never: 'I had a little taste of this literature, but only a little: now that I have gone deeper into it, I can see that what I have often read in the most serious authors is true—that Latin learning however profound is maimed, halved of its value without Greek. We have a few small brooks and muddy pools, but with them are the purest of springs and rivers running with gold.'[15]

This late start gives a certain colour to Erasmus' relationship with Greek. The translations he made from the Greek, from Lucian and Euripides for instance, were part of his effort of self-education and date from the early years of the century (Plutarch, however, he returned to as a translator late in life). The two tragedies of Euripides, *Hecuba* and *Iphigenia*, were published in 1506 by Badius and in 1507 by Aldus, but there is evidence that he was working on other translations of Euripides in 1501.[16] The translations of Lucian were also published by Badius in 1506[17] in a volume in collaboration with Thomas More, and later reprinted by Froben (1517). There were translations of Libanius too, in 1503, which he sent to an official of the Emperor's court with an apologetic air.[18] Here too it was a matter of experiment and self-teaching.

His ideas on translation are interesting. Following Cicero's rule, he thought one should attempt to translate meaning rather than words, and yet conscious of his inexperience he preferred to be conservative rather than daring. 'There is nothing more difficult than to turn good Greek into good Latin.'[19] To Archbishop Warham in the dedication of *Hecuba*[20] he describes in detail what the difficulties are: the task requires not only a good scholar in both languages but a most acute and vigilant translator, especially in such an author as this, so concise, so subtle, in whom there is nothing unnecessary and nothing can be altered without loss. And then there are those choruses, so obscure that they need an Oedipus to read their riddles; add to all this the corrupt state of the text, the lack of manuscripts, the fact that there are no other translators to fall back on. For this is a new thing to attempt, unprecedented even in Italy, and Erasmus as a *'novus interpres'* emphasizes the caution he has shown, the fact that he has tried to translate verse for verse, even word for word, preferring to be 'stuck in the coastal sandbanks rather than have to swim for it from a broken boat'. That is to say, he would rather be criticized for missing the beauty and music of the poetry than for missing the sense, and he objects to paraphrase, which is the smoke-screen thrown up by unskilful translators as the cuttle-fish throws up its cloud of darkness. This closeness in translation was abandoned in the other tragedy, *Iphigenia*,[21] and long after, in 1531, when Erasmus was discussing the difficulties of translating Plutarch, he seemed to prefer a free rather than a tight method.[22] He grew in fact to prefer paraphrase.

The choruses gave him much food for thought. It was impossible to translate them effectively, and he found them alien to his spirit. In form they provided such an excess of variety, even 'licence', that he begged to be excused for toning it down, especially as neither Horace nor Seneca had attempted to imitate it. And in content the choruses seemed to him affected and obscure.

> If my more serious studies were to allow me to translate some other tragedies, I should not only be unashamed of my daring (in toning down the choruses) but I should not be afraid to make changes in the Chorus style and matter. I would rather treat of some common topic, or go off into a pleasant digression, than spend my time on melodious nonsense, as Horace says. It seems to me that Antiquity was never more inept than in producing choruses like these; there is too much effort to be original, it ruins the eloquence, and in the hunt for verbal miracles all judgment of realities is lost.[23]

Verborum miracula—that perhaps was not a bad way of describing the wild and colourful choruses of Euripides, but Erasmus' distaste for them is perhaps a measure of the distance between his mind and some central aspects of the Greek spirit. He looked for other qualities, more rational, more everyday, more directly concerned with ethical teaching. He began to translate the *Podagra* of Lucian, but gave it up because of the style of the choruses; giving examples from Homer and Lucian[24] he declared that Latin could not give anything but a shadow of the Greek. However, he continued to translate a good many dialogues of Lucian for the sake of increasing his own dexterity. 'These trifles,' he recalls, 'won a great deal of applause at first from interested readers, but when the knowledge of Greek began to be commonly widespread among the general public, which has really happened by a wonderful advance in our country, these translations began to be neglected. I expected this, and rejoice that it is so.'

Lucian drew him strongly, both at this time (1506) and later. In 1512 he could still say, 'It was in him that Antiquity most delighted me ... for nothing commonplace could come out of Lucian.'[25] This enemy of the philosophers, touching everything with his wit, painting the ways and habits of mankind as if with a brush, speaking truth in jest, was entirely after his own heart, and had much to do with Erasmus' own jesting. 'These dialogues are better than any comedy or any satire, whether you are looking for pleasure or profit.'[26]

Apart from the perennial additions to the *Adagia*, the one Greek author whom he continued to translate was Plutarch. In 1513 he dedicated a treatise to Henry VIII ('How to Distinguish between Flatterer and Friend', suitable reading for a king). In 1525 he was writing in the preface to two small treatises (on Anger and Curiosity) that he found more and more profit in reading Plutarch. Like Montaigne, Erasmus could live in daily contact with him, relishing his learning, his knowledge of human nature, his style. 'Socrates brought philosophy down from heaven to earth, Plutarch took it into the bedchamber and the living-room of the private individual.'[27] Plutarch is 'without any doubt the most learned writer among the Greeks'.[28] To Wolsey, in another dedication, he wrote: 'This is a small book, but to put its praise in a nutshell, it is Plutarch's—and no man ever came out of Greece, that fertile mother of great minds, who was more learned or more charming as a writer. And I hardly think anyone else combined such eloquence with such accurate knowledge of affairs. When he speaks, nothing but jewels drop from his mouth.'[29] But he is difficult, particularly the *Moralia*: 'You would hardly believe how much work this little book cost me, not so much because Plutarch is rather difficult owing to his style and the infinity of things he treats, but more because he is at one and the same time the most learned of all and the most corrupt as to text, and just as he is the one most worth reading, so he is the one least possible to read.'[30]

In 1531, writing to William, Duke of Cleves, about the *Apophthegmata*[31] which he was publishing then with Froben, he discusses the value of Plutarch as a purveyor of *Sententiae*, so precious to people who have very little time, like princes. This charming dedication sums up a good many of the opinions of Erasmus about the classics, and indeed those of his time. He looks to them for practical use and knows that his generation will seize avidly on a short cut to knowledge. He thinks he should not translate but interpret Plutarch.

> Firstly because this will make for clearer speech, not closely constricted by the actual terms used in Greek. For these are not written for Trajan, a man practised in both Greek and Latin literature and in long experience of affairs, but for a young Prince, and in you for all other boys and youths aspiring to liberal studies; and not for that time, when words and deeds of this sort were well known and often told in the baths, at banquets and in the market-place.

It will also permit him to glide over obscure passages and textual difficulties, so frequent in a text so corrupt.

What comes out of the letter is Erasmus' deep sense of the value of Plutarch, and of the need to suit the book to the people for whom it was intended: his aim was to be as complete as possible but not too long, and to serve up his banquet as light fare (the following year he continued with the promised second helping, a further book of *Apophthegmata* addressed to the same William of Cleves). The letter ends with a witty defence of laughter as a condiment to learning, and recommends merry tales as the best way to teach children. After all, what are the *Moralia* of Plutarch, but curtains of coloured tapestry? The very things which seem most absurd show their serious side by the way they are treated: *ridendo discimus*.

Truth in jest, lampooning of the pompous, clear pictures of the way men behave—that was Lucian for Erasmus, and in Plutarch he found a wide serene vision of the world, high moral principles and psychological subtlety.

III

With the Greek authors he was often breaking new ground; with the Latin ones it was more a matter of restoring the text of writings that had always been known, but were in such a bad state, or so interspersed with glosses and irrelevant matter that they were scarcely their true selves at all.

He was more at home with Latin than with Greek, and certainly more at home with the Latin poets. Here he was like a man walking in his own country. From time to time he gives us glimpses of what they meant to him, and notes changes in his opinions and appreciation. In the dialogue *Ciceronianus*, one of the characters who is apparently the mouthpiece of Erasmus himself describes the pleasure he took as a boy in poetry; but as soon as he got to know Horace, all the other poets paled beside him. 'Why? Because of some hidden kinship of mind, which was apparent even in the silent pages of a book.' Virgil is less quoted than Homer in the *Adagia*, and Horace more than Homer. Ovid was regarded as child's play by Erasmus, if we are to judge by the charming preface to the poem *Nux* (attributed to Ovid) addressed to the son of Thomas More in 1523, where he talks about old men going back to children's games, and suggests that John might share the Nut with his three sisters, whose busy lives divided between music and literature are graphically sketched.[32] 'To show you I'm a boy again', he wrote to another correspondent, 'I've finished Ovid's *Nux*.'

Like Montaigne later on, Erasmus as a boy had taken great pleasure in Latin comedy. He is said to have learnt the whole of Terence by heart, and when he published a volume of Terence in 1532 it was dedicated to two boys, sons of Severin Boner of Poland, governor of the castle of Cracow. John and Stanislaus Boner were fourteen and seven at this time, and in writing to them Erasmus recollects his own youth: 'I congratulate you, my dear boys, on being born in a century which has seen new life given to true piety and better learning. For when I was a boy religion was mixed with a good deal of superstition, and in the schools the young learnt—with agony—hardly anything except what was to be unlearnt.' There are two things which really need learning, piety and liberal disciplines, which may not be virtues in themselves but prepare the mind for virtue. Nothing, he says with humanistic optimism, is more according to nature than virtue and learning, and if you take these two away from a man, he ceases to be a man at all. Here Terence comes in, 'for no other author can teach one better the purity of Roman speech, nor is any pleasanter to read or more suited to young minds'. He is better than any rhetorician, with his inventiveness in argument and readiness in response. 'There is more exact knowledge in one comedy of Terence (save the mark) than in the whole of Plautus.'[33]

Perhaps the most interesting remarks in the *Prefaces* are on Cicero and Seneca, as they show changes of opinion on Erasmus' part.

As a boy he had preferred Seneca to Cicero,[34] possibly owing to the strong influence exerted by Jerome, who thought Seneca 'the only non-Christian writer fit to be read by Christians'.[35] Nevertheless, he had published an edition of Cicero's *De Officiis*, in Paris, with the editor of the first *Adagia* Johannes Philippi.[36] The edition is not dated, but a tentative date is given to the preface by Allen, 1501. It is a formal literary letter addressed to Erasmus' friend Voecht (Jacobus Tutor) of Antwerp, referring to their shared love of study with the characteristic phrase, 'in human affairs if there is anything durable at all it is literature', and passing on from a mention of the textual difficulties to a final exordium in praise of Cicero. But this is rather stilted, as if the writer's heart was not involved in his comparison of Cicero's book with the weapons forged by Vulcan for Achilles in Homer, or for Aeneas in Virgil, or to the herb moly which gave protection against Circe's spells; or in the recommendation to search in Cicero for the Golden Bough.

Very different is the letter he wrote to the same friend in a preface to a new edition of the *De Officiis* in September 1519.[37] In conversational mood, he begins by saying that the relaxation of the true *studiosus* is yet more study, on the 'hair of the dog' principle: just as a soldier in winter quarters spends his leisure in sports and exercises which make him all the better fitted for his duty.

> For instance, when lately my health required me to refresh and restore my constitution, tired out with long and unmitigated study, I left Louvain and took a tour round some of the towns of Brabant and Flanders, so as to get away from books for a while and take pleasure in the sight and conversation of my scholarly

friends. But I could not be entirely cut off from my beloved
library, so I took a few books as companions for the journey, so
that if by chance I did not find any congenial fellow-travellers in
the coach, I should not lack someone whose conversation would
beguile the tedium of the hours. Among these I took Cicero, *De
Officiis*, Lelius and Cato, with the paradoxes of the Stoics. One
motive was the smallness of the volume, which didn't add much to
the weight of my luggage. From this, my dear Tutor, I derived
double profit. Firstly it brought back to me our early friendship,
than which there could have been nothing sweeter, and this gave
me unbelievable pleasure; and secondly it kindled in me such a
love of what is fine and good, that I never felt anything like it
before when reading our modern writers—who, Christians themselves, talk about the mysteries of Christian philosophy with great
subtlety, as we think, but with dullness just as great.

I don't know what happens to other people, I am just saying
candidly what happens to me, whether they or I am wrong. As I
read I said to myself: 'Is this a pagan writing for pagans, a worldly
man writing for the worldly? And yet in his philosophy of life how
much uprightness there is, how much holiness, sincerity and truth;
everything according to nature, nothing counterfeit or apathetic!
What an attitude of mind he demands in those who run the state!
What a picture of virtue, to be loved and admired, he puts before
our eyes! He has so much to say, and he says it in so saintly a fashion
about helping others, preserving friendship, about the immortal-
ity of the soul, and the contempt of those things for which people
will do and bear anything nowadays—and this means not only the
general run of Christians, but theologians and monks too. It makes
us ashamed of our ways; we have the teaching of Holy Scripture,
we have so many examples and promised rewards before us, and
yet we only profess the Gospel, we don't follow it.'

Erasmus was always preoccupied as he read the Classics with this
comparison. How was it that the pre-Christian writers could
express ideals so much higher than Christian practice? The
answer of course was not far to seek: that Christian practice is far
from Christian precept, that we have deviated from the simplicity
of the Gospels, and that it is when these writers are in harmony
with the Gospels that we can admire them and learn from them.
Listen to him in a later preface, still talking about Cicero.[38]

He explains that it was owing to John Froben's intention of
publishing the *Tusculanae Quaestiones*, and at his request, that
Cicero had again come up among subjects for study. 'I am glad of
this,' wrote Erasmus, 'because it is some years since I have had
much commerce with the Muses.' This rereading was valuable not

only for rubbing the rust off his pen, useful as that was, but 'for moderating and controlling the mind's desires'. (One wonders what lay behind this remark: in 1523 Erasmus was unwillingly bringing himself to write against Luther, and it was becoming obvious that the dream of a new Golden Age was fading, founded as it had been on the hope of a peaceful harmony between the regained Gospel and the New Learning.) As he read, Erasmus marvelled at Cicero's greatness, his sensitivity in treating of the past, his meditations on man's true happiness, which bore the marks of having been acted upon as well as taught, his understanding of the Greeks and his facility in using the Roman tongue to treat subjects which had seemed too difficult for it; his keenness and candour and variety and charm. How stupid people are, said Erasmus, when they go on saying that there is nothing great in Cicero apart from the trappings of language! He wrote these books in a most difficult and violent period of history. Does it not make us ashamed of ourselves when we see men like this, using the leisure thrust upon them by public disaster in this way? Not trying to distract their minds with foolish pleasures, but looking for a remedy in the holy precepts of philosophy?

It sounds like a sad allusion to the disappointing tumults of the writer's own time, but he is so far from climbing down from his earlier confidence in the sanctity of the classics that he goes on:

> How it strikes others I cannot tell; for my part, as I read Cicero, especially when he is speaking of the good life, he makes such an impression on me that I cannot doubt that the heart from which all this came was divinely inspired. And this judgment of mine attracts me all the more when I reflect on the immensity, the measurelessness of the goodness of God; which, it seems to me, some people are trying to force into too narrow a conception, simply according to their own ideas. Where the soul of Cicero walks now, it is perhaps not for human insight to decide. But I for one would not be against the views of those who hope that he is at peace in heaven. ... Never did I more agree with the judgment of Quintilian: the man who has really begun to appreciate Cicero may be sure he has made progress. When I was a boy I liked Cicero less than Seneca, and I was twenty before I could bear to read him for long, though I liked almost everything else. Whether I have got wiser as I got older, I don't know; but certainly Cicero never pleased me more, even when I was passionately taken up with those studies, than he has pleased me now that I am an old man; not only because of the wonderful felicity of his style, but because of the uprightness of his scholar's heart.

14

Turning to Seneca, we find that Erasmus' interest in him shows a converse process, rather like that of Montaigne, and throws some light on his dealings with texts that had been familiar to the Middle Ages. With ruthless good sense he prunes away pious medieval illusions.

His early enthusiasm for Seneca, inspired partly by Jerome, is reflected in the preface to the *Lucubrationes* (1515)[39] of which he had found an old manuscript at Cambridge; he took the prepared edition to Froben to be printed in Basle. Seneca was the only pagan writer to be included by Jerome in his Catalogue of authors, not so much, says Erasmus, on account of the supposed correspondence between Seneca and St Paul (Jerome was too keen-scented a critic not to have recognized its inauthenticity) but for the character of Seneca himself. No one ever took him up without being the better for it, Erasmus agrees to that. But his approval is not uncritical; he is no longer the boy reading for the first time. He finds in Seneca some commonness of diction, a certain elderly verbosity, tasteless jokes, an abrupt style. More important is the self-sufficiency which made Seneca so harsh a critic of others; 'It is remarkable to see how few people he agrees with, how many he holds up to ridicule, as it were from superior heights.'

When the time came to write a preface to a new edition of Seneca in 1529[40] these thoughts were crystallized. This is a long preface, full of interesting views about Seneca himself, his supposed relations with Christianity, and the state of the MSS. The correspondence with St Paul, long accepted as genuine, was included in this edition with a separate preface[41] pointing out the reasons for considering it fictitious. These letters are unworthy of either of these great writers, and whoever wrote them did so to persuade the world that Seneca was a Christian; even Jerome connived at this pious fraud. On the very face of it they stand condemned, by style and content alike. Imagine Seneca sending Paul a book to improve his Latin style! Could he not write in Greek? Imagine Paul agreeing to a clandestine exchange of letters for fear of Nero, Paul who was the boldest of all proclaimers of the Gospel! Would a Christian commit suicide like Seneca, and praise his wife for doing the same? 'Even in dying he dared not name the name of Christ? But I am spending too much time on this trifling affair.' Why was the suggestion that Seneca was a Christian ever made? To make Christians read his books? 'I think it is in the reader's interest to read Seneca's works as those of a man ignorant of our religion. For if you read him as a pagan, he wrote Christianly; if as a Christian, he wrote paganly.' Many things in him are far from Christian truth. 'He says the wise man owes his happiness to himself alone, and has no need of the gods, indeed that the gods themselves owe something to the sage. But our faith tells us that sparrows and lilies are in the hand of God; and that man has nothing good in himself, but owes everything in the way of happiness to the free gift of Providence.' The self-confidence of the Stoic was as alien to the mature Erasmus as to the mature Montaigne.

Erasmus finds criticisms of Seneca in Quintilian, Suetonius, Aulus Gellius; Tacitus was kinder to him. Certainly Seneca was a harsh critic of others, and not always free from the faults he censured in them, such as scurrility. There is a grace in laughter, but Seneca's is more like a snigger. He is given to bombast too, *grandiloquentia*, but this is a result of his oratorical training. Erasmus seeks to understand and account for this touch of pomposity; the habit of speaking to an audience tends to destroy simplicity.

This preface reads like a critical essay, written out of long experience and striving to be just. It touches on the question of the authorship of the Tragedies, and the suggestion that they are by the son or brother of the philosopher: Erasmus contents himself by saying they appear to him to be not all the work of one hand. Speaking of the state of the text, he gives careful and sometimes enthusiastic tribute to other scholars whose work has helped him, among them Rudolph Agricola: 'It was incredible how many good guesses were made by that remarkable man, *quam multa divinarit vir ille plane divinus*.' The fact remains that all are dealing with a most corrupt text, not only owing to scribal errors, but to two other causes, the character of Seneca's own style and the fact that the early Christians took him over as their own. Scribal errors can be detected, they always have some trace of the original about them, but mishandling by ignorant teachers produces chaos. What they did not know or recognize they were obliged to gloss over or invent, for, says Erasmus darkly, 'it is disgraceful to be silent when once you have got up into the professor's chair, and for anyone who has the dignity of the academic cap and the master's degree to admit ignorance, is really quite unfitting'. He adds: 'After all, the enthusiasm of Christians allowed Seneca to survive, when so many other famous writers have been lost; that is, if you can call this survival.'

In this edition there were also included a number of *sententiae* attributed to Seneca, but only partly collected over the centuries from his works.[42] The little preface to this section illustrates the same effort to disentangle antiquity from the adhesions of centuries.

> I found this little MS, at Cambridge, clearly written on vellum, with initial letters in colour and gold, but terribly corrupt. Some notes have been added, Heaven knows how absurd. They 'belonged to neither heaven nor earth' as the proverb says. To each note was added a hexameter, apparently explaining the same idea in different words, for the sake of showing off versatility, I suppose. Rubbish like this was lectured upon to grown men, the minds of children were tormented with such nonsense. And today there are those who resent the reinstating in schools of language study and good literature!

IV

The foregoing quotation links two subjects which were closely united in Erasmus' mind: the task of producing an emended text and the task of disseminating it, particularly to the young. He was more of a popularizer than a textual critic. In fact, although he spent much of his life on the search for true readings, he was often reduced to guesswork. The MSS were corrupt, and nothing like a full range of versions of a text could be obtained; palaeography as it is now known was not yet invented, nor textual criticism in the modern sense. 'For what can you do? There is nothing for it but to make a guess, when the authors give one no help.'[43] But in any case his interest would have lain on the practical side. We cannot imagine Erasmus as a scholar patiently dedicated to the techniques of his craft and to them alone. In many of these prefaces we see the enthusiasm for the work of restoration linked continually with hopes for the young, with the vision of a new age. 'What riches, if only one could be a boy again, *O divitias, si liceat repubescere!*'[44]

It is remarkable how many of these editions of the classics were dedicated to boys. Aristotle to John More; the *Apophthegmata* to William of Cleves; Demosthenes to John Paugartner; Livy to Charles Blount; Terence to the Boner brothers. The encouragement of the new generation was largely dependent on the work of rediscovery. Writing to Charles Blount, the son of his old patron Mountjoy, in 1531, Erasmus describes the finding of a MS of Livy (the first five books of the fifth decade) in the monastery of Lorsch.[45] This MS he says, was written in the ancient style in continuous script (*perpetua litterarum serie*) 'so that it would be difficult for anyone to separate one word from another unless he were learned and attentive and practised in this very art.' What hopes were there of finding the rest of Livy? Rumour said the Danes, the Poles, the Germans, had parts lying hidden away. If only important men would further such research by offering incentives and prizes! How much better to turn to this kind of exploration instead of delving for treasure in the earth! To some extent the co-operation of printer and editor took the place of such patronage, and Erasmus reverts time after time to the praises of the great presses.[46] The restoring of the *Natural History* of Pliny is described dramatically in the preface of 1525. If only there could be a general team-effort by the 'princes of literature', each making his own contribution, until Pliny was possessed in perfection! 'There is no small prize to be gained; for one place emended will guarantee an honourable position for that scholar's name in the memory of the studious.'

It was one of the paradoxes of Erasmus' life that this interest in the young should be a strong and continuous motive, while he had a distaste for teaching itself. He stopped taking pupils at the first possible moment, as soon as his income was assured from other sources, the English benefice or the appointment as councillor to the Emperor. Yet most of his original writings had their beginning in the penurious years of teaching in Paris, and two of the most important, the *Adagia* and the *Colloquies*, actually began as aids to students whom he taught in those years. One is reminded of the reply given by Archbishop Warham to the objection that his protégé Erasmus was an absentee Rector of Aldington: 'He will do better work for the Church by his absence than his presence.' Similarly, Erasmus had to cease to be a pedagogue before he became important as an educationist. But the impulse to teach was strong in him.

The prefaces echo the tone of his educational writings, the *De ratione studii* and the *De pueris instituendis*.[47] The advice to learners in the *De ratione studii* gives a graded list of classical authors: 'The Greek prose-writers whom I advise are in order, Lucian, Demosthenes, Herodotus, the poets, Aristophanes, Homer, Euripides; Menander if we possessed his works would take precedence of all three. Amongst Roman writers, in prose and verse, Terence for pure terse Latinity has no rival, and his plays are never dull. I see no objection to adding carefully chosen comedies of Plautus. Next I place Virgil, then Horace; Cicero and Caesar follow closely, and Sallust after these.'[48] These are the authors who provide both interesting matter and elegance of style. Later in the treatise we find recommendations on where to look for information of a practical kind, in Pliny, Macrobius, Aulus Gellius and Athenaeus; for ancient wisdom, in Plato, Aristotle, Theophrastus and Plotinus and the Fathers of the Church; for the mythology which underlies the poets, in Homer, Hesiod, Ovid and the modern Boccaccio; for geography, so important for understanding literature, there is Pomponius Mela as a compendium, Pliny and Ptolemy and Strabo. As the pupil increases his grasp, he is led to literary criticism with the help of such masters as Cicero, Quintilian and Seneca. In Erasmus' own dealings with the problems of education, Plutarch and Quintilian are important sources, together with a favourite mine of Greek quotations and proverbs, Diogenes Laertius.[49]

The essential thing about the presentation of these authors is that they should be graded to suit the reader, because education depends on a sympathetic understanding of the pupil, and it should be made enjoyable, not a hateful task. With keen recollection of his own boyhood, Erasmus proposes attractive roads to learning, even games and prizes, and puts before his schoolboy no dry lists of grammatical mnemonics but a lively, expansive panorama of the wisdom of the past.

His relations with his classical authors are marked by a strong critical spirit exercised with good sense and fairness, and an unswerving confidence in truth, with the touch of excitement which spurs on the discoverer. In the *Adagia* one sometimes catches a whiff of the intoxication of those days, when he mentions the 'poem about Spring' which Aldus showed him, freshly unearthed from an old library in France (the *Pervigilium Veneris*) or describes the MSS which poured into the Aldine Press from distant places, Hungary or Poland for instance, and the generosity of scholars who offered him help on every side with the task of hurrying into print the riches which had been the possession of the few.[50]

Erasmus and his contemporaries were not only working for the erudite, not only concerned with emending texts and stocking libraries; they were building up a new view of the past, differentiating between the centuries and obtaining a perspective which had been unknown to the medieval mind.

V

The chief means of doing this, as far as Erasmus was concerned, was the *Adages*. Begun as a small collection of proverbs, mainly Latin, but utilizing some of the Greek collections, the book blossomed into Thousands of Proverbs (*Adagiorum Chiliades*). Erasmus increased it every few years, and it became a kind of 'commonplace book', an anthology of prose and poetry with comments picking out points of scholarship, or details from the daily life of the ancient world, or leading to a philosophic idea or to a discussion of the burning questions of the day. The Greek quotations were always translated into Latin so the book became a kind of Greek reader as well. One saying might call up a rule of Pythagoras, another a dialogue of Plato, another might draw a striking parallel between the wisdom of the ancients and the commands of Christ, another would tell a joke or comment on the continuity through the ages of children's games. The *Adages* made the past as vivid as the present and showed the links between the two. It turned to specialists for specialized information, to Vitruvius for architecture, Columella for agriculture, Vegetius for military history, Strabo for geographical detail. It ranged in time from Homer and Hesiod to the compilations of Medieval writers such as Suidas and Eustathius. Some of the greatest writers, like Lucretius, barely figure in the *Adages*, though on the whole poets and philosophers are much more quoted than historians, but this is in the nature of a book centred on proverbs: Suetonius, Livy, Herodotus appear rarely in these pages, Tacitus only three times. But proverbial sayings are rife in poets and playwrights, and the oft-recurring names in the *Adages* are those of Aristophanes, Euripides, Homer, Lucian, Horace, Plautus, Terence, Virgil; side by side with them, Aristotle and Plato, Cicero and Plutarch, and the elder Pliny.

Along with these the *Adages* find room for some 250 other authors, mostly ancient, though there are a few mentions of

Renaissance scholars or of post-classical compilations. On the whole the range of classical allusions was fixed by the first large edition of the *Adages* printed by Aldus in Venice in 1508, though in later editions it is sometimes clear that a new book has come to his notice; for instance, all the references to the *Table-talk* (*Deipnosophistae*) of Athenaeus date from after 1514 when the Aldine edition of the Greek text was printed. The extensive additions to the *Adages* which Erasmus made towards the end of his life (especially in 1533) show some differences; there is a marked increase in quotations from Cicero, as we should expect, and a return to Plautus, a renewed interest in Sophocles, and less attention to the former favourites Homer, Lucian, Plutarch, Horace, Terence. Sometimes a long run of quotations from one source suggest that they mark Erasmus' current reading. The plan was loose enough for him simply to add new proverbs, and it was only very occasionally that he changed one from place to place or inserted another. What he did do was to insert new material in the body of the existing comments, carefully dovetailing so that the enlargement of the passage could not be detected except by comparison with the preceding edition. The treatment of each adage followed a general scheme: the proverb itself came first, usually in Latin, next its Greek equivalent, then its elementary meaning, its use by classical writers, sometimes with a discussion on variants of language or interpretation; finally its wider significance or symbolism, and its application to modern times. Erasmus seems to have prepared a basic list with scholarly details and then, nearer the time for going to press, to have added stories or personal comments of his own. This method was so elastic that it gave every possibility of using a wide range of reading and linking up with the present. No wonder the new editions were eagerly looked for, and a reader who could not afford the next one went to the labour of copying in the margins of his treasured volume all the latest tit-bits, and on the fly-leaves all the additional proverbs.

In a foreword to the edition of 1533[51] Erasmus jokingly suggested that perhaps the time had come when the reader might cry 'Stop, that's enough!', rather than welcome new additions to the *Adages*, and for various reasons the author might feel inclined to agree. Such an enterprise, he said, could take all one's time, 'especially now that the ancient writers who were previously lying hidden are emerging into the light.' One might very well prefer to spend one's old age on subjects more decent to 'die in', and one might feel that 'these flowerets and gems with which learned writers are wont to decorate their works have perhaps more charm when the reader picks them out for himself, from authors who have not been vulgarized by passing through many hands, instead of taking them from well-worn collections of this sort.' However the Greeks did not look at it this way, nor do the present-day printers. And so there was to be yet another edition of the *Adages*.

This book had an effect on the middle years of the sixteenth century of which one finds traces everywhere, though its full extent must remain incalculable. It had begun as a student's handbook and after Erasmus' death it reverted to something of the same kind, both in the *Epitomes* which began to be made even in his own lifetime, and which he welcomed as an aid to the young student, and in new editions containing work of other hands. At this level the book supplied an easy road to a cursory knowledge of the classical authors, and a magazine of ammunition for moralist and preacher. At a more evolved level, its effect on Rabelais may be taken as a good example. The *Adages* are quoted liberally in the five books of *Pantagruel*, and sometimes in such close juxtaposition as to make it quite clear that Rabelais was using them as a short cut to the Classics, accomplished scholar though he may himself have been. But it was not only a matter of quick access to suitable sources. Rabelais' use of the *Adages* springs from a deeper level, from a profound similarity in outlook. And this was not only because Rabelais agreed with Erasmus on the 'middle way' which fused together Evangelistic reform and classical humanism. He also shared Erasmus' view on the continuity of life. The ancient writers, like the ancient proverbs, were not to be divorced from the present; the users of proverbs in Rabelais are people like Panurge or Frère Jean, that is to say the least secluded or stilted of people; they are the down-to-earth characters who speak the language of everyday and of the common man. A proverb was the crystallization of experience, and its recurrence linked the generations. So proverbs to Rabelais as to Erasmus were the authentic human voice, often coming out of far antiquity but still with the ring of popular speech.

This brings us to a subject that was much debated in the sixteenth century: the place of Latin as a learned or a popular language, and the consequences of attempting to put the clock back and reinstate classical Latin as a universal tongue. Like other humanists, Erasmus despised the modern vernaculars. But there are signs in the *Adages* that just as he was conscious of the links between his classical proverbs and the common European stock of sayings which had subsisted into the vernacular, he also sometimes tried to relate modern words to their classical parentage. He refers to vernacular proverbs from time to time, usually Dutch or French ones; where the ancients said, 'You could light a lantern at his anger' the modern Dutchman said, 'You could have cooked an egg on his forehead.'[52] In his latest additions to the *Adages* these references become perhaps more frequent. And sometimes he makes (quite erroneously) an effort to trace the classical origins of words:

> II.ix.v. *Ter* (three) is used as a magic number in Greece; there is a relic of this use in French, where they use TRE to make a comparative or superlative (Très?).
>
> II.iv.lxxii. *Betizare*. In this passage there is a mention of the word Blitea as a term of abuse meaning stupid. 'It may be that the French are still using this word when they commonly call the lowest and most despised men Bliteros, adding just one letter.' (??)
>
> IV.vi.lxv. φελλίνας. This means cork, and is used to mean anything light or worthless. 'The English language today has a word for an easy-going and untroublesome man—they call him φελλέα (fellow?).'

Certainly Erasmus regarded the modern European languages as corruptions of the classical, and had all the scorn of the humanist for medieval Latin. He would not have read *Gargantua*, but the dog-Latin of Maitre Janotus de Bragmardo would have been a joke after his own heart. On the other hand he strongly resisted every tendency to divorce the past from the present, and he saw a real danger in the attempt to impose a pedantic purism on the current use of Latin. Here the affair of the *Ciceronianus* can be seen in focus with the aims of the *Adages*. He had put his utmost efforts into restoring the elegance and versatility of Latin, in order to make it fit for all modern purposes as a universal tongue. This very effort was to defeat its own ends, as the more literary Latin became the less it was likely to compete successfully with the vernaculars. Erasmus saw the red light when the 'Ciceronians' attempted to restrict Latin to the narrowest classical forms. As usual, he saw safety in the middle way.

The *Ciceronianus* is a dialogue between three speakers, Nosoponus (the name means a man suffering from an illness), Bulephorus (the counsellor), and Hypologus (the thoughtful witness). It puts the case against Cicero-worship in the manner of the *Colloquies*, at first with comic exaggeration and then with a serious attempt to define what the relationship should be between a modern writer and his classical models.

Nosoponus explains to his friends that he is ill, pining away from the desire of fame, the fame of a Ciceronian. How does he seek to achieve it? In several ways:

(1) By making a dictionary of all the words and phrases used by Cicero.

(2) By not admitting even other cases or forms of these words if they are not found in Cicero (those actually in Cicero are marked in red, the others in black).

(3) By shutting himself up in a library as if in a padded cell, remote from the world.

(4) By keeping his mind free from all other cares. He takes no public post or position of responsibility, and he remains a bachelor.

(5) By having no dinner and only a light lunch on days when he wishes to study. Ten small currants and three coriander seeds will do.

(6) By choosing his nights for study by horoscope, and he has bought a book on astrology for the purpose.

(7) By spending a night on each paragraph and writing it ten times over.

(8) By using French and German for ordinary occasions and keeping Ciceronian Latin for best.

(9) By marking out set Ciceronian phrases for certain events.

This light-hearted caricature set Erasmus' world by the ears, especially as a passage further on suggested that the French scholar Longueil was among modern Ciceronians. *A cheval*, as ever, on the subject of national prestige, a section of French readers protested violently. But with his usual forethought Erasmus had taken care to make fun of himself.

BULEPHORUS (*on contemporary scholars*): I'll suggest Erasmus Roterodamus if you like.

NOSOPONUS: You said you were going to talk of *writers*! Far from numbering him among the Ciceronians, I don't even count him a writer at all.

The dialogue soon settles down into a serious discussion on what was then a burning problem, and Bulephorus points out how unrealistic it is to try to stretch Cicero's vocabulary and phrases to fit the modern world. Even dating a letter 'after Christ' must necessarily be un-Ciceronian. It is important for Christians to speak as Christians, and let Cicero speak as a pagan to pagans. 'How many matters are there which come up in our talk daily and of which Cicero never even dreamt? But if he lived with us he would talk as we do.' His style cannot suit all subjects. Even if it did, some reservations must be made. Elegance can be bought too dearly. Variety is important. More important still is the need for speech to be a mirror of the soul. 'What pleases the reader best is to feel as if he knows the feelings, character, intellect and outlook of the writer as well as if he had spent several years in his company.'[53]

The important subject Bulephorus reaches is the question of imitation or assimilation of the classical models. Cicero himself set us an example in the way of picking out the best for his models, and we must do the same. Like du Bellay in his *Deffence et Illustration* Erasmus has a clear idea of what imitation should do.

> I approve of imitation, not of one chosen author from whom one dare not stray by a line, but imitation of anything which is excellent in itself and in harmony with your own mind; it should not be a matter of attaching to your speech whatever pretty thing turns up, but of assimilating it in your soul as the stomach assimilates food and passes it into the veins, so that it may seem born of you, rather than begged from another, and may carry with it the force and character of your own mind and nature; so that he who reads will not recognize a thought stolen from Cicero, but will see instead the child sprung from your own brain like Pallas from the head of Jove, a living image of its parent.[54]

As in other connections, Erasmus was pleading for the spirit rather than the letter. Literature is a living force, and the present can learn from the past without being its slave.

VI

Steeping oneself in the classics was thus to have a deep and far-reaching result, not the mere parrot-talk of conventional copying. Erasmus was not only a scholar and popularizer of the classics, he was also the author of some of the most original works of his century, and in these a delicate question arises: how did such *jeux d'esprit* as the *Praise of Folly* and the *Colloquies* relate to the Classical background? Erasmus was the great publicist of the Classics in his time, and surely not least in those books which were in everyone's hands? The longer essays in the *Adages*, even the *Letters* contributed to the encouragement of a certain attitude of mind. It may be worth while to try to summarize a few of the characteristics of this side of his work.

First, as to the direct imitation of Classical forms. Erasmus was a poet in his youth and an enthusiastic student of Latin prosody,[55] but this cannot be said to have had much influence on his contemporaries. The use of the dialogue was the most important element he took from the Classics, notably of course from Lucian, though there are many Platonic echoes. When he recast the first book of the *Antibarbari* it was to give it a Socratic setting, like that of the *Phaedrus*, transplanting the plane tree by the Ilissus into a garden in Holland where his good Dutch friends, James Batt the town clerk of Bergen and William Herman the poet, sat discussing the resistance of their time to the winds of change. There are signs of the Socratic method in the *Colloquies*.

In the *Adages* one long essay, *Scarabeus aquilam quaerit*, opens with a burlesque imitation of an epic in the grand manner, with Homeric similes and invocation of the Muses, and ends with an account of the council of Jove.[56] The *Praise of Folly* itself is a declamation in a set form, with many Classical prototypes both as to structure and subject: the semi-facetious preface addressed to More refers the reader to a series of parallels in ancient literature, from Homer (Battle of the Frogs and Mice) Virgil and Ovid to Lucian, Plutarch and Apuleius, with a final fling at the last will and testament of a pig mentioned by Jerome.

The *Praise of Folly* comes nearest to a flight of fancy of all Erasmus' writings, and yet it is serious in aim and scope and full of psychological acuteness. Perhaps one of its attractions for its own day, as for us, was its timelessness. If the idea of a burlesque encomium was from classical models, the declamatory form suggested a favourite activity of the medieval schools, and the review of human types ranging from women to Popes smacked of the moralizing of the *Danse Macabre*. But the ironical spirit was classical and modern. It was after his visit to Italy that Erasmus gave rein to his talent for irony, with perhaps a thought of Roman satire, so old and yet so new, and of the posters on the statue of Pasquino. Irony sprang from a certain form of self-consciousness, an awareness of the complications of life, a sense of the elusive nature of truth, and it was a kind of coming of age which was celebrated by the *Praise of Folly*.

It was no accident that Erasmus, who recoiled from the chorus in Euripides, should take for his models the more practical writings of the ancients, and it was particularly the dialogue which satisfied his taste for acute observation and the analysis of real experience. It was a form which allowed for epigrammatic conciseness, a special excellence of his own style. Neither speculation nor fancy were uppermost here; Erasmus never wrote stories, and he had nothing but contempt for the current vernacular literature such as the romances of chivalry. Literature was to amuse, yes, but it was also a two-edged weapon for the eradication of social vices and the exposure of human weakness. The *Colloquies* are in a sense the destructive side of an effort which had its positive effects in the ideals put forward in the *Enchiridion*. And yet the *Colloquies* have their affirmations too: one has only to think of the one on Faith (*Inquisitio de fide*) with its solemn and beautiful exposition of Christian doctrine, or the conversation between the friend of the family and the young mother (*Puerpera*) expressing advanced views on the bringing up of children. More than any, perhaps, the Godly Feast (*Convivium Religiosum*) embodies the blend of classical and Christian idealism.

A group of friends converse in a garden, to the sound of the fountain and among the scent of flowers, and their host shows them round the house with its galleries, painted with trees and birds like the walls of a Roman room, and entertains them to a rural meal during which they discuss passages of the Bible—the *Book of Proverbs, Isaiah, Hosea, I Corinthians*. Their talk opens the door to the classics.[57]

> CHRYSOGLOTTUS: If I weren't afraid my chatter would interfere with your eating, and I thought it lawful to introduce anything from profane writers into such religious conversation, I'd present something that didn't puzzle but delighted me extremely as I was reading today.
>
> EUSEBIUS: On the contrary, whatever is devout and contributes to good morals should not be called profane. Sacred Scripture is of course the basic authority in everything; yet I sometimes run across ancient sayings or pagan writings—even the poets'—so

purely and reverently and admirably expressed that I can't help believing their authors' hearts were moved by some divine power. And perhaps the spirit of Christ is more widespread than we understand, and the company of saints includes many not in our calendar. Speaking frankly among friends, I can't read Cicero's *De senectute*, *De amicitia*, *De officiis*, *De Tusculanis Quaestionibus* without sometimes kissing the book and blessing that pure heart, divinely inspired as it was. But when on the other hand I read these modern writers on government, economics or ethics—good Lord, how dull they are by comparison! And what lack of feeling they seem to have for what they write! So that I would much rather let all of Scotus and others of his sort perish than the books of a single Cicero or Plutarch.

The *Colloquies* suggest an inexhaustible fund of interest in the vagaries of human nature, and it is this individualism which strikes such a modern note. Often in his letters, too, Erasmus speaks with a sudden spontaneous naturalness which brings him to our elbow. Spontaneous, yes, but it was part of the method; the conscious aim expressed in the *Ciceronianus* to let the full flavour of personality impregnate the written page. It is perhaps in this that the influence of the classical spirit is most clearly expressed. The Renaissance speaks to us now because it learnt from the ancients a potent modern truth, embodied in the phrase from Terence which Montaigne wrote on a beam in his library: *Homo sum*, I am a man, and nothing human is alien to me. The ironical dance of fools through the pages of the *Praise of Folly*, the crowd of characters which jostle in the *Colloquies*, are looked at with a quizzical but not unsympathetic eye—except when there is a topical axe to grind. The value and variety of people, the shimmering canvas of the world, are real, significant and precious to these heirs of a new antiquity: or as another lover of the classics said, *the creature hath a purpose, and its eyes are bright with it.*[58]

NOTES

A large proportion of the notes throughout this book refer to P. S. Allen (ed.), *Opus Epistolarum Des. Erasmi Roterodamu*, Oxford University Press, 1906–1958. Where applicable, volume and page numbers are given; otherwise, the number of the letter will be found in parentheses.

[1] *Erasmi Epistolae*, ed. P. S. and H. M. Allen (492).
[2] *Ibid.*, I. p. 2. (To John Botzheim).
[3] *Ibid.* (1110).

[4] *Ibid.*, I. p. 2.
[5] *Ibid.* (1).
[6] *Ibid.*, I. p. 47. The attribution to Erasmus is not certain.
[7] *Adagia*, I.iv.xxxix.
[8] Allen (3032).
[9] *Ibid.* (20).
[10] *Ibid.*, *Op. cit.*, Index.
[11] *Ibid.* (123).
[12] *Ibid.* (124).
[13] *Ibid.* (131).
[14] *Ibid.* (131n.).
[15] *Ibid.* (149).
[16] *Ibid.* (158n.).
[17] *Ibid.* (187).
[18] *Ibid.* (177).
[19] *Ibid.* (177).
[20] *Ibid.* (188).
[21] *Ibid.* (208).
[22] *Ibid.* (2431).
[23] *Ibid.* (208).
[24] *Ibid.*, I. p. 7.
[25] *Ibid.* (267).
[26] *Ibid.* (193).
[27] *Ibid.* (1572).
[28] *Ibid.* (272).
[29] *Ibid.* (284).
[30] *Ibid.* (268).
[31] *Ibid.* (2431).
[32] *Ibid.* (1402).
[33] *Ibid.* (2584).
[34] *Ibid.* (1390).
[35] *Ibid.* (325).
[36] *Ibid.* (152).
[37] *Ibid.* (1013).
[38] *Ibid.* (1390).
[39] *Ibid.* (325).
[40] *Ibid.* (2091).
[41] *Ibid.* (2092).
[42] *Ibid.* (2132).
[43] *Adagia*, IV.iv.lxxv.
[44] Allen (643).
[45] *Ibid.* (2435).
[46] *Ibid.* (648, 1544).
[47] *De pueris statim ac liberaliter instituendis*, ed. J.-C. Margolin, Droz, Geneva 1966.
[48] Woodward, W. H., *Desiderius Erasmus concerning education*, Cambridge, 1904, p. 66.
[49] Margolin, *op. cit.*, p. 89–101.

[50] M. M. Phillips, *Adages of Erasmus*, Cambridge, 1964, p. 186; A. Renaudet, *Erasme et l'Italie*, 1954, p. 84.

[51] Allen (2773).

[52] *Adagia*, IV.x.lxxvii.

[53] *Ciceronianus*, Froben, 1528, p. 405.

[54] *Ibid.*, p. 408.

[55] C. Reedijk, *Poems of Erasmus*, Leiden, 1956.

[56] Phillips, *Adages*, p. 229 ss.

[57] *Colloquies*, tr. Craig R. Thompson, Chicago, 1965, p. 65.

[58] Keats, *Letters*, March 19th 1819.

II

Erasmus as a Satirist

A. E. DOUGLAS

I

SATIRE, unless it be defined as the works which their authors
have at any time called satires (which is of no help for the present
purpose), occupies a territory with ill-defined frontiers between
serious moral discourse or homily on the one hand, and on the
other invective or lampoon, direct verbal assault on named or
easily identifiable individual persons. The former overlaps with
satire when it makes ridicule its weapon, the latter when a general
moral purpose and again the element of ridicule (but not ridicule
alone: exaggeration and fantasy seem to be proper to satirical
invective) can be detected. Of satirical invective against individuals
Erasmus is hardly to be counted a practitioner. Even if only out of
nervousness he eschewed such attacks, preferring to keep in
reserve the satirist's escape-hatch 'If the cap fits . . .' Of the one
possible example of personal invective, the *Julius Exclusus*, he
would, in modern official phrase, neither confirm nor deny his
authorship. But across the other border-zone, where solemn
homily meets satire, Erasmus moves freely and frequently. Indeed
while *Julius Exclusus* is doubtful in authorship and in taste,
Erasmus' one certain contribution to sustained satirical writing,
the *Praise of Folly*, is, we shall see, but partially successful; it is in
the short aside or digression or the brief commentary, that is
generally on a small scale and often in a non-satirical context,
that his satirical gifts are best seen. We may begin by considering
why this is so.

Juvenal, founder of satire in the modern sense, puzzles his
readers by an apparent lack of moral centre, by seeming at least, to
take the most famous example, to equate Nero's matricide with his

musical extravagances. One sees that either the writer's moral standards are gravely confused or that he is satirizing the confusion of moral standards in others, but because Juvenal's uniformity of manner makes no evident distinction in severity between the moral turpitude of matricide and aestheticism, we cannot be sure which. A recent writer[1] attempts to solve, or abolish, the problem by seeing in Juvenal's satires, literary exercises in rhetorical point and wit. Whether or not Juvenal was so little concerned with his actual subject-matter as this theory might allow one to deduce, certainly he *was* setting himself consciously to write satire. If the will to write in the genre and not in fact the allegedly unexampled wickedness of the times was Juvenal's main impulse, we can understand why his moral centre remains in doubt.

Erasmus is a different case. When he attempted the literary exercise in satire, he wrote too fast to write really well. When Erasmus' satire is good, it is when it is used as but one weapon among many, to achieve a clear moral or intellectual end, and not as an end in itself, a literary form to be played with. With him, as he claimed, the satirical manner is subservient to the moral purpose. He does not merely set himself to write satire, come what may: he writes satirically when satire is the right weapon. Erasmus knows on the one hand that moral deficiencies may be too grave to be merely ridiculous; on the other hand he has an acute sense of what *is* merely ridiculous. Mankind is guilty of crimes as well as follies, and his crimes may outstrip the range of even the most mordant ridicule; yet the grimmest of human offences may include as subordinate elements absurdities and incongruities which can be proper objects of satire. But Erasmus is seldom concerned with confining himself to one or other aspect of human behaviour, his eye is on the situation in all its aspects; hence his frequent changes of tone and mood.

There is an obvious example in Erasmus' attitude to war. War for him was certainly no joke, yet satire is not lacking in his writings on war. He repeatedly fastens with ridicule as well as straightforward indignation on the incongruity of militant Christendom, the moral incoherence of a society which hangs the brigand and glorifies the plundering soldier:

> Infamis est qui vestem furto sustulit; qui et proficiscens in militiam et militans et rediens a militia tot immeritos spoliavit inter probos cives habetur. (II. 962 E.)

The man who steals a garment is disgraced: one who on his way to the war and during the fighting and on his way back home plunders so many innocent folk is regarded as an admirable member of the community.

Or he may tilt at the triviality of the causes of war:

Nos, Deum immortalem, quam frivolis de causis quas bellorum Tragoedias excitamus! Ob inanissimos ditionis titulos, ob puerilem iram, ob interceptam mulierculam, ob causas his quoque multo magis ridiculas. (II. 964 B.)

How frivolous are the reasons, Immortal God, for which we stir up the catastrophes of war! For the emptiest claims to sovereignty, because of childish passion, or the kidnapping of a wench, or for reasons far sillier still.

Or again from the same source (the long commentary on the adage *Dulce bellum inexpertis*), the *reductio ad absurdum* of one motive for war, and a satirical statement of real motives:

Repetant scilicet hodie Patavini Troianum solum ... repetant Africam et Hispaniam Romani. ... Vide porro quam non magna res agitur. Non illud decertatur, ut haec aut illa civitas bono principi pareat potius quam tyranno serviat, sed utrum Ferdinandi censeatur titulo an Sigismundi, Philippo censum pendat an Lodovico. Hoc est illud egregium ius ob quod universus orbis bellis caedibusque miscetur. (II. 965 B.)

Why, the Paduans should now reclaim the soil of Troy, the Romans Africa and Spain. ... But come now, consider how trifling the issue is. The motive of the conflict is not to ensure that this or that community should be subject to a good prince rather than enslaved to a despot, but whether it is to rank as part of the dominions of Ferdinand or Sigismund, pay taxes to Philip or Louis. These are the noble 'rights' for which the whole world is torn with war and bloodshed.

II

Erasmus' satire gains much by being written on a basis of firm conviction. Though he is sometimes lacking in the literary arts of the greatest satirists, he is preserved from their two besetting sins. One is the common ambivalence of being half in love with what one professes to hate, by which the satirist defeats his own ends, if these really are moral censure and not the expression of a general disgust with human life, or literary gymnastics. However unconvincing the surrounding context, Erasmus in his preface to the

Praise of Folly strikes this nail on the head in saying that, unlike Juvenal, he will describe the *ridenda* rather than the *foeda*, the laughable rather than the filthy; or again in the *Adages* (*Ollas ostentare*), he writes in defence of the *Praise of Folly* that from Juvenal readers learn how to criticize,

> principum, sacerdotum, negotiatorum, ac praecipue mulierum vitia . . . quae saepius ita depingunt ut obscoenitatem doceant. (II. 461 D.)

> the vices of rulers, priests, businessmen, and especially women . . . which they often so depict as to instruct in obscenity.

Sexual excess and perversion had been a stock subject for satirists from ancient times, but the most we have from Erasmus is a little gentle mockery of feminine foibles in a mood very different from that of Juvenal's sixth satire, to say nothing of his second. In an age like the present, which already shows signs of finding comic its own freedom in discussion and behaviour, one should hesitate to attribute Erasmus' restraint to mere prudery.

The other fault is of course indiscriminate destructiveness. While the satirist's method is necessarily critical—if he explicitly advances moral teaching to a significant extent, he becomes a preacher—*épater les bourgeois* is not really a very subtle or satisfying aim; nor is the 'professional' satirist's pose that everything human is merely ridiculous or contemptible, nothing sublime or satanic, less self-defeating than the trap of ambivalence. Indeed the strength of Erasmus' satire lies precisely in the lack of that pose. That he appealed even in satirical moments (we are not yet dealing with mere light-hearted banter of satirical quality: Erasmus' achievement in this field we shall consider later) to a firm moral centre, and a particular moral centre, helps to explain the hostility that his works aroused—and still arouse. His sheer efficiency as a writer, his enormous learning and fluency, provide, of course, part of the explanation of the bitterness he provoked: no one likes to feel helpless under a hail of ridicule. But more serious offence was given precisely by his persistent probing of what seemed to him the incongruity between Christian practices of his day and the teaching of the Gospel. The objects of his bitterest attacks could not retort with a *tu quoque* as Horace's victims had done ('Have you no faults'?),[2] nor with a generalized, 'That's the way of the world'. Any satire implies some assumption of moral or intellectual superiority: yet the fact that Erasmus' implied claim is only to a clearer vision of the meaning of Christianity both lessens the arrogance and adds sharpness. Most of us would rather be by implication involved in general criticisms of the standards of society at large than constantly reminded of failure to live up to those standards which we actually profess. Even when assaulting intellectual excesses, of scholasticism in its decadence or extravagant Ciceronianism, his intention is to contrast pedantries with Christian simplicity and seriousness. His most consistently powerful satire is directed in fact not at those acknowledged by everyday standards as vicious—too easy targets—nor at groups he fortuitously disliked (though he can be amusing about these), but on those he saw as at best misunderstanding, at worst wilfully hypocritical about, the standards demanded by Christianity.

A further illustration. The rich and avaricious, the birth-proud, were derided by satirists long before Erasmus, partly because satirists have often been poor men, and more seriously because these targets can be shown to have misunderstood the true sources and values of human well-being. Erasmus satirizes them too, greed and hauteur being ridiculous rather than (in themselves) wicked:

> Semideus habetur qui sanguinis seriem ad Codrum Athenicnsem aut ad Brutum Troianum, qui haud scio an unquam natus fuerit, aut ad fabulosum Herculem referre possit: et obscurus est qui sibi litteris et virtute famam paravit? Illustris est cuius tritavus in bello strenuum praestitit homicidam: et plebeius est atque imaginibus caret qui bonis animi profuit orbi? (II. 774 E.)

> Do we reckon a demigod the man who traces his lineage to Codrus of Athens or Brut the Trojan (who for all I know never existed) or the legendary Hercules, and leave in obscurity him who once made a name through literature or moral worth? Is he a man of note whose great-great-grandfather showed himself in war a valiant murderer, the man whose mental gifts have benefited the world lowly and undistinguished?

But again Erasmus appeals to a moral centre which, as is not the case with many satirists, can easily be identified as the simplicity of Christ and the Gospel:

> Quorsum igitur opus fuit harum rerum accessione quas tot incommoditates comitantur? An vereris ne parum potens futurus sit Christus propriis opibus nisi laicus tyrannus aliquid impertiat suae potestatis? Parum ornatum putas nisi profanus bellator aurum,

phrygionem, candidos mannos et satellitium illi indulserit, hoc est aliquid de suo fastu asperserit? (II. 780 E–781 A.)

What was the point of the acquisition of these things which are attended by so many disadvantages? Can you be afraid that Christ will be too weak in his own strength unless a secular despot bestows something of his power? Do you think him insufficiently adorned unless a profane man of war grants him gold, and a goldsmith, gleaming carriage-horses and a retinue, that is, a share of his own luxury and pride?

Is this not more effective than merely jeering at a man for being rich, or (even) newly rich?

III

Just as, from our initial point of view, satire occupies a zone contiguous and partly overlapping with homily and invective, so in intensity it may vary from (i) passages of light-hearted criticism through (ii) passages of satirical manner but clearly serious intent, to (iii) passages in grave contexts where one reader may detect a flash of irony and ridicule, and another (or even that same reader in a different mood) only indignation and passion. We have been considering why Erasmus is particularly liable to offer passages of this third type, so presenting a certain problem to a contributor to a symposium who may feel an obligation not to stray too far beyond his assignment.

In this last category (we shall consider the three in reverse order) one may put much of what Erasmus wrote at length about war, notably the adage *Dulce bellum inexpertis* and the *Querimonia Pacis*. Is there a curl of the lip or pure anger in such passages as the following onslaught on Christian involvement in war?

> Denique quod ego sane puto his omnibus atrocius, Christianus cum homine: addam invitus, quod est atrocissimum, Christianus cum Christiano: et o caecitatem mentis humanae! Haec nemo miratur, nemo detestatur. Sunt qui applaudant, qui vehant laudibus, qui rem plus quam Tartaream, sanctam appellent ac principes ultro furentes instigent, oleum, quod aiunt, addentes camino. Alius e sacro suggesto promittit omnium admissorum condonationem, qui sub eius principis signis pugnarint. Alius clamat, Invictissime Princeps, tu modo serva mentem istam religioni faventem, Deus pugnabit pro te. (II. 956 E.)

Lastly, what I think more appalling than all this, the Christian (fights) with his fellow-man: I must add reluctantly the most

36

appalling thing of all, Christian with fellow-Christian: and such is
the blindness of the human mind, nobody is surprised at this,
nobody execrates it. There are people who applaud, who extol,
who call 'holy' this worse than hellish business, and who spur on
princes who need no incitement to insanity, adding, as they say,
'oil to the flames'. One man from the holy pulpit promises forgive-
ness of all sins to those who fight under the standards of that
Prince. Another cries, O most invincible Prince, do you but preserve
your devotion to religion, and God will fight on your side.

Erasmus goes on to say that some distort Biblical quotations in the
interests of the combatants, but then any hint of satire gives way,
most characteristically, to tremendous solemn anger:

> Concurrunt acies utrimque crucis insigne praeferentes, quae vel
> ipsa poterat admonere quo pacto conveniat vincere Christiano. A
> sacro illo caelesti, quo perfecta illa et ineffabilis Christianorum
> coniunctio repraesentatur, curritur ad mutuam caedem. . . . (II.
> 957 B.)

> The battle-lines clash, both sides bearing before them the sign of
> the Cross, which of itself should suffice to show in what fashion
> Christians should gain their victories. From that heavenly rite in
> which is shown forth the perfect and ineffable unity of Christians
> they rush to mutual slaughter.

In the *Complaint of Peace* irony can be clearly heard in the passage
where Erasmus contrasts the shame of submitting to a neighbouring ruler with the real shame of supporting one's self against him
by alien alliances:

> At quanto humilius deicis maiestatem tuam dum barbaris cohor-
> tibus et infimae sceleratorum farci numquam explendae auro
> subinde litare cogeris, dum ad Cares vilissimos simul ac nocentis-
> simos blandus ac supplex mittis legatos, dum tuum ipsius caput,
> dum tuorum fortunas illorum credis fidei, quibus nihil est neque
> pensi neque sancti! (IV. 640 B.)

> But how much lower you degrade your majesty when you are
> compelled to do obeisance to the troops of the barbarians and the
> lowest criminal dregs who can never be sated with gold, when you
> send envoys with smooth supplications to the Carians, the most
> worthless and withal most villainous of men, when you entrust
> your very life and the fortunes of your kindred to the good faith
> of those who hold nothing in respect, nothing holy.

And again:

> Quorum inventum est bombarda? Nonne Christianorum? Et quo
> res fit indignior, his induuntur Apostoli nomina, insculpuntur
> Divorum imagines. O crudelis irrisio! Paulus ille pacis hortator

perpetuus Tartaream machinam torquet in Christianum? Si
cupimus Turcas ad Christi fidem adducere, prius ipsi simus Christiani. (IV. 640 E–F.)

Who invented the cannon? Christians, was it not? And to make
matters worse, these are given the names of an Apostle, images of
the saints are engraved upon them. O savage irony! Does Paul
(i.e. a cannon 'dedicated' to him) who ever urged peace, hurl that
hellish device at a Christian? If we want to make Christians of the
Turks, let us first be Christians ourselves.

But only a little earlier after discoursing on the quarrels of lawyers
and litigants—and here we pass to our second category—Erasmus
has dealt more lightly with a lighter matter, the quarrels of
scholars and theologians:

Si res pugionibus aut lanceis non agitur, stylis veneno tinctis sese
confodiunt, dentata charta dilacerant invicem, alter in alterius
famam letalia linguarum vibrant spicula.

Granted the fight is not with daggers or spears, they murder each
other with pens dipped in venom, they tear each other to pieces
with their fangs of paper, and one launches against another's
reputation the deadly weapon of his tongue.

Erasmus is referring of course to the violently personal tone of
theological dispute in his own, as in other, times, and for reasons
we mentioned at the outset, he perhaps avoided personalities
sufficiently not to be accused of being himself a notable and persistent marksman with the literary weapons he has thus described.
Yet he wrote much that however elegant in style, and amusing in
substance to the likeminded, was sharp and shocking enough to
many of his contemporaries. Generality of expression will not
have blunted the point of the opening of his comment on the
adage *Illotis manibus*, which is, as so often with Erasmus, all the
more effective because he has on this occasion allowed himself to
be brief and crisp:

Utrumque proverbium recte usurpabatur in eos qui vel audacius
vel parum instructi rebus his quibus oportuit negotium invadunt:
veluti si quis principis munus capessat, nulla neque sapientia neque
rerum usu praeditus; aut si Divinas litteras interpretari conetur,
Graecae Latinae et Hebraicae linguae denique et omnis antiqui-
tatis rudis et imperitus. . . . (II. 354 E.)

Both proverbs (i.e. the Greek and Latin forms) were appropriately
employed with reference to those who either with excessive boldness or without the necessary training in the relevant field engage

in an undertaking; as for instance when someone undertakes the duties of a ruler, though devoid both of wisdom and experience; or when someone attempts to expound holy scripture though untrained in and ignorant of the Greek, Latin, and Hebrew languages, and in short the whole of antiquity.

The stolid text-book manner of the passage combines with the pointed selection of illustrations to produce an effect that is more than piquant: one almost senses a pent-up savagery.

Perhaps the best known of Erasmus' exercises in bitter comedy is the colloquy *Naufragium* (*The Shipwreck*). The behaviour of the despairing crew and passengers is the vehicle for an attack on Mariolatry, the localization of the worship of the Virgin and the Saints, and other features of late medieval piety which were favourite targets of the Reformers. Thus:

> Nautae canentes, Salve Regina, implorabant matrem Virginem, appellantes eam stellam maris, reginam caeli, dominam mundi, portum salutis, aliisque multis titulis illi blandientes quos numquam illi tribuunt sacrae litterae. (I. 713 A.)

> The sailors singing 'Hail Queen of Heaven' prayed to the Virgin Mother, calling her the Star of the Sea, Queen of Heaven, Mistress of the World, Haven of Salvation, and cajoling her with many other titles which the holy scriptures never attribute to her.

> ADOLPHUS: Aderat Anglus quidam qui promittebat montes aureos Virgini Walsingamiae si vivus attigisset terram: alii multa promittebant ligno crucis quod esset in tali loco: alii rursum quod esset in tali loco. Idem factum est de Maria virgine, quae regnat in multis locis: et putant votum irritum nisi locum exprimas
> . . .
> ANTONIUS: Ridiculum quasi divi non habitent in caelis. (Ib. B-C.)

> ADOLPHUS: There was an Englishman there who promised mountains of gold to the Virgin of Walsingham should he reach land alive. Others promised great gifts to the wood of the Cross in such-and-such a place; others to the Cross in such another place. The same happened in the case of the Virgin Mary, who is queen in many places: and they think the vow invalid unless you name the places explicitly.
> ANTONIUS: Absurd—as if the saints do not dwell in heaven.

Only the narrator Adolphus dares to address his prayers directly to God:

> ADOLPHUS: Recta adibam ipsum patrem dicens, Pater noster qui es in coelis. Nemo divorum illo citius audit aut libentius donat quod petitur. . . . (714 A.)

39

ADOLPHUS: I approached the Father Himself directly, saying, Our Father which art in heaven. None of the saints is quicker than He to give hearing, or more gladly grants our requests. . . .

ANTONIUS: Quid actum est de Dominicano? AD. Is, ut idem narrabat implorata divorum ope, abiectis vestibus, nudum se commisit natationi . . . ANT. Quos divos invocabat? AD. Dominicum, Thomam, Vincentium et nescio quem Petrum, sed inprimis fidebat Catharinae Senensi. ANT. Christus illi non veniebat in mentem? AD. Ita narrabat sacrificus. ANT. Melius enatasset si non abiecisset sacrum cucullum: ea deposita qui potuit illum agnoscere Catharina Senensis? (I. 715 B.)

ANTONIUS: What happened to the Dominican? AD. He, my informant said, besought the help of the saints, took off his clothes, and plunged naked into the sea. ANT. What saints did he invoke? AD. Dominic, Thomas, Vincent, and some Peter or other, but above all he relied on Catherine of Siena. ANT. Didn't he bethink himself of Christ? AD. So the priest said. ANT. He would have been more successful if he hadn't taken off his hood. Once he removed that, how could Catherine of Siena recognize him?

There is lastly the generally good-humoured satire aimed at the temporarily vexatious phenomena of everyday life such as tax-collectors, bad inns and so forth. Here the vexation may certainly be real, but it is not profound: Erasmus' attitude corresponds. The adage *A mortuo* (I.ix.12) is so amusing and still so topical on various forms of avarice that it is worth quoting at some length:

Vina non importantur nisi saepius decimata. Non recondis in cellam nisi dimidium aut certe quadrantem totius pretii seces Harpyiis illis sceleratissimis. Apud quosdam ex cervisia, quam vocant, plus quam dimidii seponitur principi. . . . Non revendis equum tuo emptum aere, nisi penderis aliquid . . . nec modus est nec finis, quotidie novas exigendi vias excogitant, et quicquid semel invasit per occasionem temporis id mordicus retinent. (II. 337 F.)

Wine cannot be imported without the payment of several dues. You do not put in your cellar without chopping off half or at any rate a quarter of its whole value for the benefit of those villainous Harpies. With some people 'beer' (as they call it) pays a tax of more than fifty per cent to the King . . . you cannot resell a horse, bought with your own money, without paying something. There is no bound nor limit, every day they think up new forms of exaction, and whatever has once been introduced to meet a momentary need they hang on to like grim death.

Erasmus, of course, never forgave the English customs who, at Dover in 1500, practised on him the Tudor form of exchange control, and relieved him of a large sum of gold. Taxes on beer and wine are still with us, and modern examples of the process referred to in the last words of the extract are too numerous to quote: exceptions are harder to think of. Erasmus would doubtless appreciate the habit of recent Chancellors of the Exchequer of describing the invariable perpetuation of allegedly temporary and emergency imposts as 'consolidation'. Erasmus then passes to another inevitable target, payments to clergy:

> Non datur baptismus, hoc est non licet fieri Christianus, nisi numeres: atque his praeclarissimis auspiciis fores ingrederis Ecclesiae . . . Sed quod apud istos gratuitum fit, apud quos emitur et sepultura, etiam in alieno solo? Apud ethnicos miserae plebi stabat commune sepulcrum: erat ubi gratis quos velles sepelires. Apud Christianos nec mortuis operiri terra licet nisi a sacerdote tantulum spatii conduxeris et pro pretii modo dabitur locus amplus et magnificus. Si plurimum numeraris, in templo proxime summum altare licebit putrescere: si parce dederis, inter plebeios sub dio complueris.

> Baptism is not granted, that is, you may not become a Christian, unless you pay: and with these noble auspices you enter the doors of the Church. . . . But what can you get free from those people, from whom even burial must be bought, even if it be in some one else's land? Among the heathen 'there was a common burial ground for the poverty-stricken plebs' (Erasmus is quoting Horace *Sat.* i.8.10)—there was somewhere you could bury whom you wished for nothing. Among the Christians the dead may not be covered with earth unless you rent the tiny plot from a priest and for a certain sum you will be granted a broad and splendid site. If you pay the top price, you will be allowed a place in the church by the high altar, in which to rot: if you pay only a little, you will lie among the common herd with the rain falling on you under the open sky.

The last sentence, which is brief (only eighteen words in the Latin) and bitter (note the irony of the delayed *putrescere*), shows that Erasmus is not merely fooling; but one may still detect that this is not the solemn invective which he directs at those who discredit their religion by making war or pervert its fundamental doctrines.

We may close this discussion of Erasmus as satirist in a lighter mood (on the whole) by referring to his criticism in the *Colloquies* (I. 849) of a popular compendium which claimed to teach all knowledge in a fortnight:

> Ego aliam artem notoriam non novi nisi curam, amorem, et assiduitatem.

I know of no other Art of Knowledge than the taking of pains, love of the subject, and perseverance.[3]

or to his comment on a not dissimilar theme, the adage *Ignavis semper feriae sunt* ('It's always Bank Holiday for the lazy'). This adage might not seem to allow of much comment, even from the fluent Erasmus, and indeed he is here brief, pointed, and amusing:

> Ut ad proverbium revertamur, apte accommodabitur in eos qui numquam non causantur aliquid quo sint in otio: veluti quibus insuaves sunt litterae, nunc excusant valetudinem, nunc occupationem rei domesticae: nonnumquam obstat rigor hiemis, alias aestatis fervor, interdum autumni periculosum caelum. Demum avocat a libris veris amoenitas mox fugitura. Pransi negant esse rem habendam cum libris antequam concoxerit stomachus. Impransis obstrepit fames quo minus libeat. Luci dicunt ignavum esse domi desidere, ceterum ad lucernam vigilare oculis inimicum. Si suppetit res domestica, quorsum opus, inquiunt, litteris? Si deest, negant pauperem posse philosophari. Iuvenis negat aevi florem curis senilibus absumendum: provectior ait valetudini parcendum. (II. 586 E.)

> To return to the proverb, it is appropriate to those who invariably have an excuse for being idle. For instance, those who find literature distasteful, now plead ill-health, now pressure of family business. Sometimes the rigours of winter are the obstacle, at other times the heat of summer, between whiles the unhealthy weather of autumn, and the final distraction from books is the charm of spring, so quick to pass. Those who have dined say they cannot attend to books until they have digested: those who have *not* dined are prevented by hunger from wanting to. By day they say it is lazy to sit around indoors, but to stay awake by the lamp is bad for the eyes. If they are well off, what, they say, do you need literature for? If they're not, they say a poor man can't be a philosopher. The young man refuses to waste the prime of life on old men's concerns: when he is older, he says he must watch his health.

IV

It would have been a pity to leave aside the effective light-hearted ridicule in which Erasmus sometimes indulged. But it was of course the first two types of satire that gave Erasmus a reputation as a biting and dangerous critic of contemporary ecclesiastical doctrines and practices. To those mentioned already could be added from the *Colloquia* alone criticisms of pilgrimages, indulgences, and the prohibition of meat-eating on Fridays and other fasts.

Naturally the orthodox were suspicious and hostile, the Reformers impatient at his refusal to identify himself openly with their cause. Where Erasmus actually stood and whether on any particular matter he was right or wrong are questions which, in so far as this is a literary study, do not concern us here. Just as there is clearly a sense (though idealists like Cicero and some moralists since his time have denied it) in which a bad man can be a 'good' orator, so a bad or misguided man can be in a technical sense a good, that is to say, effective satirist. However greatly cherished or revered were the beliefs, practices and institutions that he attacks, we may still ask whether he writes well or ill. The extent to which he shocks and hurts is indeed one (not the only) measure of his effectiveness. Yet in Erasmus' case the matter cannot quite be left here. We have seen that we are not dealing with literary exercises. If a satirist is plainly as serious as Erasmus usually is, the question of whether he is right or wrong may be of some importance. It is worth considering why in Erasmus' case it has come to seem peculiarly important.

Erasmus' satire at the expense of Pope, clergy and the Church generally, is naturally associated in most minds with the tremendous upheavals of the Reformation period. Yet there was a long tradition of such criticism, sometimes more savage than Erasmus and even by modern standards blasphemous, something which (for reasons we need not reiterate) Erasmus never was. Criticism of the Roman Church as an institution, above all the Roman Curia for its greed, and of monks and friars, is a recurrent theme of medieval satire. Nor of course did secular authority escape satirical censure on similar grounds. Even now that vigorous side of medieval writing is not perhaps as familiar as it might be: but many will have encountered (not, probably, without a sense of shock) the 'Gospel of the Marks of Silver', a cento of scriptural phraseology scandalously devised as a weapon to assail the greed of the Papal officials; and the world of the Archpoet and the other 'followers of Golias' is not distinguished by respect for the forms and institutions of established religion.[4] There is much too in less deliberately outrageous vein. Bernard of Cluny's De contemptu mundi, a metrical *tour de force* in pure dactylic rhyming hexameters, attacks the worldliness of the clergy, the violence of soldiers, the greed and dishonesty of farmers, and with references to ancient Roman satirists, the avaricious and rich in general. To the same vigorously satirical age, the twelfth century, belongs Nigel Wireker's *Speculum Stultorum*, the tale of the disillusioning travels of Brunellus the ass: the work assaults all the monastic orders one by one, and kings, bishops, and laity. Gilles de Corbeil in his diffuse but often lively work and Jordan of Osnabrück are others who somewhat later carried on the tradition of satirizing the dignitaries of the Church.

We cannot now look in detail at the whole field of satire in the developing European vernaculars, which culminated in Erasmus' own day in Brant's *Ship of Fools*. But it is worth recalling that G. R. Owst explored and expounded the literary sub-world of the late medieval (vernacular English) sermon. He showed that in those sermons many ideas and moods found expression for which students of the period had been too willing to trace high literary pedigrees but which in fact were simply in the late medieval air for anyone to encounter and exploit: among those ideas and moods the satirical play no small part.[5] Among the victims of these attacks by clergy are (above all) the Church and clergy themselves. (In Owst's view the Church's prestige was thus greatly weakened from within, long before the emergence of the Reformation movement in the usual sense of the term.)

Yet when all this is said, Erasmus cannot easily be separated from his time as a figure of Renaissance and Reformation. He is a Renaissance figure in that while he shows the influence of Renaissance writers like Poggio and Valla, his debt to medieval satirists is scarcely traceable, nor would he at all have countenanced association with the more scurrilous of the writers alluded to above. The brief dialogue of Barbaria and Thalia which will be discussed later shows what he thought of medieval Latin versification: and the major medieval satires are in verse. He owed much of course to the Roman satirists, Horace, Persius and Juvenal, and in this resembled his medieval predecessors from Adalbero of Laon in the tenth century and Egbert of Liège in the eleventh with their many reminiscences of the Roman writers, who were also well known to the twelfth-century writers of lyrics *cum auctoritate*, like Walter of Chatillon, to whom they frequently provided the borrowed tags that conclude their stanzas. But he owed more to a writer his forerunners did not know, the Greek prose-satirist Lucian, many of whose works Erasmus translated into Latin. His debt is evident in the crisp and vivid dialogue of some of the

Colloquia: the Greek, one of the most entertaining of ancient writers, was a master of this form, and he too, unlike the Romans (except perhaps Juvenal in his tenth satire on the proper objects of prayer), attacked the intellectual and moral weaknesses of contemporary religion and its adherents as well as many other manifestations of the bogus, pretentious and hypocritical. If Erasmus has Christian models, he is in a tradition of Christian writing as old as St Jerome (if not St Paul), with his scathing denunciations of worldly Christianity.

Erasmus is a figure of the Reformation period not only in this appeal to the early Church. In his day not only the Church as an institution, but also the defects of its human representatives were, as so often before, under attack. Its religious practices and doctrines were under fire as never before, and though Erasmus was conservative about the Church's doctrine in the narrow sense, his other criticisms (on indulgences, auricular confession and so forth) certainly had theological implications. That is why it is still not easy to judge Erasmus as a satirist without taking into account whether one agrees with him or not.

V

It is time to turn from Erasmus' occasional use of satire within larger contexts to his purely satirical works, the *Praise of Folly* and *Julius Exclusus*. With these may be considered the *Ciceronianus*, for even though here as so often Erasmus' satirical criticisms give way to a serious and positive consideration of the issues involved and the procedures to be recommended, the work coheres as an attack on a single well-defined target.

The *Praise of Folly* was written very fast, within a week, though there is evidence that Erasmus, like Mozart, may have spent a good deal of time shaping his endlessly fertile ideas in his head before actually putting pen to paper—and it should perhaps be read fast too. For it scarcely bears close analysis. In it Folly delivers an oration on her own behalf, a fact which at once suggests a conflation of two forms anciently held distinct. Satire the work certainly is, and is intended to be, as Erasmus' preface and later defence (on *Ollas ostentare cf.* above) show. But it is also descended from a curious ancient form of *oratory* which may be called the paradoxical encomium (the Greco-Latin title of Erasmus' book is

Encomium Moriae), in which the writer exercised all his art and skill in defending the indefensible.[6] It was originally intended as an exercise in ingenuity, which should demonstrate the powers of oratory even with an unpromising subject: it was not satirical, but rather paradoxical or ironical, and since Erasmus fails to observe this distinction, it is of some importance that we for the present purpose should.

It has often been pointed out that for all its brilliant passages and incidental flashes of wit, the *Praise of Folly* suffers from a fundamental incoherence, and this incoherence results precisely from the combination in it of everything that can paradoxically (i.e. untruthfully) be said on behalf of Folly, with everything that Folly can say by way of satirizing the real follies of mankind. This conflation of forms and approaches is perhaps more genuinely the source of the incoherence than the reason more commonly alleged: that Erasmus has entangled himself in the logical complexities of having Folly (who must not be believed) as the speaker. When Folly speaks of real human follies, she should defend them, and leave the reader to take the point, but too often Erasmus (not Folly) is clearly the speaker, and the half-hearted attempts to save the situation, which will be illustrated shortly, are altogether unconvincing, both aesthetically and as an attempt to save Erasmus from the odium which his (not Folly's) attacks—most of them were on familiar enough Erasmian themes—were bound to invite. It was also, of course, futile for Erasmus to try to defend himself by claiming that in so far as he was directly satirical he was *merely* writing in the ancient tradition of satire, of Greek Old Comedy and Lucian, and must therefore not be taken too seriously: did not his ancient models intend to be taken seriously?

To illustrate from the work itself: we are first told that all the pleasures of life, success and fame, are owed to one or another kind of folly, and in the world of the paradoxical encomium this is logically satisfactory. The standards of achievement accepted are those of the everyday world, and it is for the reader to decide how far amid arguments deliberately perverse or frivolous, he must acknowledge an element of truth in the attacks on intellectualism —reason is not the whole of a human being, philosophers are ineffective in public affairs, and much more effective are foolish stories like the fable of the interdependence of the parts of the body with which Menenius Agrippa allegedly quelled an insurrection of the Roman plebs. Fools take action instead of consulting antique tomes. Human life simply would not work without the element of 'folly' which makes so much of it just a theatrical performance. Thinking leads to suicide: I, Folly, make people love life—dirty old men and lecherous old women are here vividly depicted; surely it is better to be even like this than to hang oneself. The dilemma is of course false, and 'better' must be taken in a popular sense, but the point is a genuine one, as when within the same popular frame of reference, Folly contrasts the agonies of the intellectual with the cheerful vacuity of the fool and idiot.

But it is at this point (IV. 441) that the *jeu d'esprit* gives way to satire on fools. Folly no longer utters her paradoxical half-truths. Without notice Erasmus takes over, and all the familiar targets of his scorn reappear—after cuckolds, those who build on an extravagant scale, alchemists, and gamblers, come foolish worshippers of saints and those who accepted doctrines of nicely calculated reliefs from Purgatory. At the close of this bitter passage Erasmus tries to reassert the ostensible mood of the piece: pride of birth is foolish, but it is in the context of praise of Folly, 'good'—people like it, and it makes them happy. Why bother to learn a skill? The inexpert man is more popular. Folly touches on other kinds of foolish pride, for example, sources of national pride. Then she turns to flattery: there is a valuable kind (a really valuable kind—Erasmus, not Folly, speaks). But again the focus shifts, and Folly tells us that opinions are more conducive to *felicitas*, 'happiness' as popularly understood, than is truth.

The same confusion appears in the criticisms of various social groups which begin at IV. 457 B. On the whole Erasmus speaks in the attacks on grammarians, poets, and rhetoricians, lawyers and theologians, and he can make good jokes: scholars wear bands round their heads because they are so full of rubbish that otherwise they would burst ('alioquin etiam plane dissilirent'). But again there is something unsatisfactory, though the wit is itself often good, about the sudden asides that remind us how it all began, as on monks:

Spe sua felices sunt non absque meo beneficio.

In their own expectation they are happy, not without help from me.

Or on rulers and princes, who have tremendous responsibilities but 'thanks to me (Folly)' are not unduly worried by them; or in the savage attack on cardinals and prelates: men behave as they do because they misunderstand the truth, but they are happy because they misunderstand.

Perhaps the nearest we come to a clarification of objectives or reconciliation of aims is with the statement (IV. 487) that Fortune favours the foolish and rash, but the wise are timid: wisdom is useless for *public* success. As for wealth:

> Quos uti contemnit sapiens, ita illum sedulo fugere consuerunt.

> Just as the wise man despises it, so wealth for its part invariably shuns him.

But now, as often, Erasmus turns serious, neither satirical nor paradoxical. Many citations of the praise of folly from Classical and Biblical sources serve to introduce a new theme, the contrast of Christian folly with worldly wisdom. This folly is neither the anti-intellectualist folly that ensures worldly success nor the folly of fools as the satirist sees them at work in Church and society at large. The work approaches its end with a rhapsodical eulogy of Christian folly, though to be sure before we are done, the satirical note returns in a discourse on the folly—that is, now, the eccentricities—of the pious. And if we appear to be doing Erasmus less than justice, we must confess that he realized what he had been about. Just as at the end of the vast commentary on the adage *Scarabaeus* (iii.7.1) he turns the tables on the wilting reader by pointing to criticisms of his earlier commentaries as being too brief, so the last paragraph of the *Praise of Folly* is a brief acknowledgement of the chaos of the material:

> Video vos epilogum exspectare sed nimium desipitis, siquidem arbitramini me quid dixerim etiamdum meminisse, cum tantam verborum farraginem effuderim. (IV. 504 C.)

> I see you are awaiting a peroration but you are very silly if you think I can even remember what I have said, after pouring out such a hotch-potch.

It may not be coincidental that Erasmus here refers both to an *epilogus*, the technical term in antiquity for the peroration to a *speech*, and in the same breath to a *farrago*, famous as Juvenal's description of his own *satire*.

It will be clear that one reader at least finds it amazing that the *Praise of Folly* has ever been regarded as a literary masterpiece. It reads exactly like what it is, a brilliant but artless and uneven improvization by a man of great learning and fluency of style. Few at any time could have written this work in one week, but easy writing is notoriously liable to make hard reading. In this instance the difficulty is not in detail: no better example perhaps could be found of what the ancients called *volubilitas*, the style that rolls and rushes like a river. But unless the reader simply surrenders himself to the onrush of the invective, he must constantly ask himself which sort of folly, if indeed any, is now speaking. Erasmus' contemporaries of course knew when he was serious, and admired or resented his invective and wit; they were responsive to the appeal of a virtuoso's Latinity; and we can still appreciate these aspects of the *Praise of Folly*. But it is not being humourless to judge the work inadequate by higher critical standards. And it is no help to urge that this is a mere *jeu d'esprit*, and to accuse the judicious critic of heavy-handedness. The chief fault of the *Praise of Folly* is in fact precisely the same whether one takes it as a light-hearted trifle or as a serious piece of literature. Whichever way, the *Praise of Folly* is simply far too long. The joke, which began as a pedantic pun on Moria, the Greek for Folly, and the name of Erasmus' friend Sir Thomas More, to whom the work is addressed, will not last the distance, and desperate recourses are needed to keep the theme alive even in semblance. A joke seventy-five pages long (in the latest English translation) has to be a very good joke indeed.

One adage Erasmus as a writer seems not to have taken to heart was one of the most familiar of all: Do nothing in excess. Repeatedly his excessive fluency and extravagant parades of learning blunt the edge of his satire. There is a superfluity of matter and style alike. Too frequently we are reminded that Erasmus was the author of the *Colloquia*, which has provided us with some examples of satire, but which was after all a Latin phrase-book, beginning with around fifty courteous or insulting ways of saying 'Good morning' in Latin. Take the following passage from the *Praise of Folly* on the sources of national pride:

> Iam video ... fieri ut Britanni praeter alia formam, musicam et lautas mensas proprie sibi vindicent; Scoti nobilitate et regiae affinitatis titulo neque non dialecticis argutiis sibi blandiantur:

Galli morum civilitatem sibi sumant: Parisienses Theologiae
scientiae laudes omnibus prope submotis sibi peculiariter arrogent:
Itali bonas litteras et eloquentiam asserant; atque hoc nomine sibi
suavissime blandiantur omnes quod soli mortalium barbari non
sint, etc.

It is, I see, the fact that the Britons claim as their preserve beauty,
music, and lavish banquets, the Scots esteem themselves on the
score of nobility of birth and royal connections, the French claim
'la politesse'; the Parisians claim to have the field almost entirely
to themselves in theology; the Italians lay claim to literature and
eloquence; and all take pleasure in flattering themselves that they
alone in the world are civilized.

One chooses a brief passage for reasons of space, but it suffices.
Even here one is too conscious of variations on the phrase 'claim',
'flatter themselves' etc. (*vindicent, blandiantur, sumant*, and so on).
Satire has its own rhetoric: this is not it, as we see by contrasting
such passages with Erasmus at his best:

Iam quid de proceribus aulicis commemorem? quorum plerisque
cum nihil sit addictius, servilius, insulsius, abiectius, tamen
omnium rerum primos sese videri volunt. Hac una in re tamen
modestissimi, quod contenti aurum, gemmas, purpuram, reliqua-
que virtutum ac sapientiae insignia corpore circumferre, rerum
ipsarum studium omne concedunt aliis.

Why should I say anything about courtiers? They are the most
slavish and servile, fatuous and contemptible of creatures, yet they
want to be thought lords of creation. On one point alone they are
easily contented: they are satisfied to wear on their bodies gold,
jewels, purple and the other outward symbols of virtue and
wisdom, but to leave the pursuit of what is symbolized to others.

The phrase-book is not quite absent, but it is under control. The
passage works because manner and matter balance. The scorn is
genuinely that of satire, not of invective or homily.

A last illustration. In its final form the adage *Sileni Alcibiadis* has
a passage of nineteen successive rhetorical questions (twelve with
Cur followed by seven with *Quid*), and the next page offers eleven
successive *dum*-clauses. How much more effective is the brief
commentary on *Fabarum arrosor* (II. 1085 B), where Erasmus
writes:

Nunc palam donantur ingentia praemia, qui suffragantur in creando
Summo Pontifice et Caesare. Quin et ipsi Principes quidam simpliciter vendunt magistratus, et miramur collabi civium discipli-
nam.

Now great bribes are given openly to those who elect the Lord Pope and Emperor. Why, some kings frankly put up offices of state for sale—and we are surprised that civic order is collapsing.

VI

Julius Exclusus is less famous than the *Praise of Folly* for two reasons, first, because of Erasmus' refusal to acknowledge authorship of this anonymously published work, and secondly, because this attack on the recently dead Pope Julius II—he is depicted as being refused admission to heaven by St Peter—has often seemed in poor taste. As to the first, we shall here assume the more probable of the two alternative authors suggested by contemporaries, 'Aut Erasmus aut Diabolus'.[7] The second point cannot be belittled, yet the satire, though strong, is far less cruel than that in two lampoons on similar themes, Seneca's *Apocolocyntosis* on the lately dead Emperor Claudius, and Byron's *Vision of Judgment* where George III is the victim. Indeed the modern reader may well be struck by an almost *sympathetic* quality in the satire. It is a brilliant study in mutual incomprehension. St Peter simply cannot understand what has happened to the office which he was first to hold, and humbly asks to be instructed. Julius for his part is made to seem naïvely unaware of the enormity of his behaviour as he expounds it. On his intrigues against the proposed General Council of the Church he innocently observes:

> Erat id paulo quidem impudentius, verum non patebat via commodior.

> It was a bit shameless, but no other convenient way was available to me.

Peter sympathizes:

> Oportet sceleratissimos fuisse cardinales auctores ac principes concilii.

> The cardinals who proposed and led the Council must have been utter villains.

But Julius replies that he has nothing against their characters ('De moribus non queror . . .'): it was their regrettable enthusiasm for reforming the Church which was frustrated by the timely death of the ringleader, the Cardinal of Rouen. Again:

> PETER: Num interim in te nefanda dicta scribebant?
> JULIUS: Immo furciferi hic plus sapiebant quam volebam: rem

odiosissimam mira modestia tractabant et non solum tempera-
bant a maledictis sed me numquam nisi cum honoris praefatione
nominabant.

PETER: Didn't they sometimes write unmentionable things against
you?

JULIUS: No, the blackguards had more sense here than I hoped.
They dealt with this most objectionable matter with astonishing
restraint and did not merely refrain from insults, but never
mentioned me without using honourable terms.

To Peter's lesson from the humility and sufferings of Christ,
Julius gives the blunt man's answer:

Inveniet fortassis qui laudent, qui imitentur neminem his sane
temporibus.

He will find some to praise him, but in times like these none to
imitate him.

Times have changed, he patronizingly reminds his bewildered
interlocutor:

Tu fortasse veterem illam ecclesiam adhuc somnias . . . iam aetas in
melius commutavit omnia: alia longe res nunc est Romanus
pontifex.

Perhaps you are still dreaming about that primitive church. . . .
But time has changed everything for the better: it's a very different
thing nowadays to be Bishop of Rome.

Peter eventually achieves understanding and assaults Julius with
fine rhetoric, but Julius of course cannot comprehend. You are
worse, Peter says, than the infidel Sultan.

PETER: Certe mens eadem, consimiles vitae sordes: tu maior orbis
pestis.

JULIUS: At ego cupiebam ecclesiam omnibus bonis exornatam.

PETER: Certainly you have the same outlook, the same squalor of
life but you are a worse plague to the world.

JULIUS: But I wanted to have the church adorned with all good
things.

But what *are* good things? That the Church was great in poverty
and suffering is something of which Julius declares flatly that he
has never heard. Small wonder, replies Peter, for a man like you:

tot legationibus, tot foederibus, tot rationibus, tot exercitibus, tot
triumphis occupato.

preoccupied with so many embassies, treaties, policies, armies, and
triumphs.

Much as Erasmus disliked in particular Julius' military ambitions and activities—it is his military aspect which first surprises Peter —he manages to make of him in this satire more than a victim of personal spite. Much of what Julius says condemns not only himself but aspects of the Church in general, and more than this, it is possible to ignore the ecclesiastical issue altogether, and to see Julius as any man in authority, *genuinely* concerned for the prestige of the institution he serves and of his own position within it, yet hopelessly superficial in outlook and blithely insensitive to any but material standards. Not only in Renaissance Popes do we find such objects for satire. The political, business, and academic worlds, as well as the ecclesiastical, are still able to produce examples.

VII

Lastly, a glimpse of Erasmus as satirist in literary matters. A tiny early piece presents Thalia and Barbaria, symbols respectively of Classical and late Medieval Latinity, abusing each other like two (very literate) fishwives. Towards the end of his life, Erasmus gave much fuller attention to the extreme Classicists, or rather Ciceronians, those who, almost incomprehensibly to the modern mind (since they engaged in extravagant defence of, not attacks on, a tradition), rejected from their Latin every expression not found in the works of Cicero. The first part of Erasmus' dialogue *Ciceronianus* is among his liveliest writings. Bulephorus catches sight of an old friend Nosoponus, once jolly, red faced, and inclined to portliness, but now almost wasted away by years devoted to the detailed study necessary to ensure no breach of strict Ciceronian principles. He has had of course to avoid the distractions of marriage and family life.

> BULEPHORUS: Sapuisti, Nosopone. Nam mea coniunx, si noctu parem ad istum modum operam dare Ciceroni, perrumperet ostium, laceraret indices, exureret schedas Ciceronem meditantes: et quod his etiam est intolerabilius, dum ego do operam Ciceroni, illa vicarium accerseret qui ipsi pro me operam daret. Itaque fieret ut dum ego meditor evadere Ciceroni similis, illa gigneret aliquem Bulephoro dissimilem.
>
> BULEPHORUS: Very sensible of you, Nosoponus. My wife, if I prepared to study Cicero at night the way you do, would burst in through the door, tear up the indexes, and throw on the fire the sheets of Cicero-practice. Much worse than this, while I pay

attention to Cicero, she would get a deputy to pay attention to her in my place. As a result, while I practise so as to resemble Cicero, she would produce someone not resembling Bulephorus.

Erasmus was not often as naughty as this.

NOTES

[1] J. P. Sullivan (ed.), *Critical Essays in Roman Literature: Satire*, Routledge & Kegan Paul, 1963, pp. 93ff.

[2] Horace, *Satires*, 1.3.19: 'Quid tu? Nullane habes vitia?'

[3] On the Classical and Medieval origins of the kind of quick course in memory-training here discussed, and the reasons for Erasmus' dislike of what he regarded as a kind of Medieval mumbo-jumbo, see Frances Yates, *The Art of Memory*, Routledge & Kegan Paul, 1966, especially pp. 127, 132 and 158.

[4] For a translation of the 'Gospel', see C. H. Haskins, *The Renaissance of the Twelfth Century*, Cambridge University Press, 1927, p. 185; for the Latin text, with many other shocking documents, e.g., parodies of the Mass, see P. Lehmann, *Parodistische Texte*, Munich, 1923.

[5] G. R. Owst, *Literature and Pulpit in Medieval England*, Cambridge University Press, 1953, especially chs. 5–7.

[6] On its influence during the Renaissance, see C. A. Mayer, 'Rabelais' satirical eulogy' in *François Rabelais: le quatrième centennaire de sa mort*, Geneva and Lille, 1953, pp. 147ff.

[7] Allen, *Erasmi Epistolae* (502).

III
The Letters of Erasmus

J. W. BINNS

THERE is a certain difficulty in writing about letters. They are not a branch of imaginative literature, and are now usually classed with essays and *belles lettres* as minor writings. Letters attract the most interest when they are the product of a man who was famous, usually in the political, but sometimes in the intellectual life of his times. Thus Cicero's letters have had an obvious interest for subsequent generations: they are important as a historical source, they provide glimpses of political life behind the scenes, and they show the man himself aside from his public life, rummaging in a library after a dinner party perhaps,[1] or embroiled in domestic upset.[2] They attract us since we have an interest in the man himself and in human individuality. Similarly, we read Pliny for the picture he presents of a Roman man of letters of the first century A.D., and Lady Mary Wortley Montague for a view of the eighteenth century seen through the eyes of a literate and cultivated woman. We also read letters for the pleasure of their style, which is generally urbane—the easy and conversational tone in which the writer describes the details of his daily life, and gives his views on the problems and conditions of his age, his observations on life, his view of the world.

Erasmus' letters have a self-evident historical importance. He was a strong influence on the thought and educational theory of his day, and he was drawn into the controversies which led up to the Reformation. His correspondents included popes and kings, archbishops, and princes—the spiritual and temporal rulers of Europe of every degree. Erasmus' letters are not only a valuable source for historians, but they also provide vital information for any biography of the man. It is not this aspect which I wish to discuss here, however. I propose instead to try to show that Erasmus' letters possess claims on our attention over and above their value as historical documents. In the first place Erasmus is worthy of note as a writer of Latin prose in the wider realm of Latin literature which continued long after the fall of the Roman Empire until the end of the Renaissance. An appreciation of Erasmus' letters has been hindered by the very number of them that survive, which obscure through their profusion the ones that are most remarkable. For Erasmus was a prolific writer of letters throughout his life. Those which survive today fill 1,932 columns in the great Leyden edition of Erasmus' works,[3] and eleven volumes in the complete edition by P. S. Allen,[4] although both these editions include some letters addressed *to* Erasmus. About 1,600 of Erasmus' own letters survive. Erasmus himself referred to the great number of his letters in his *Catalogus Lucubrationum*:

> Epistolarum tantum scripsimus et hodie scribimus, ut oneri ferendo duo vix plaustra sint futura paria. Ipse multas casu nactus exussi, nam sensi servari a compluribus.[5]

> I have written, and am still writing today, such a mass of letters that two waggons would hardly be equal to carrying the load. I myself, having come into possession of many of them by chance, burned them, for I realized that they were being preserved by very many people.

Again, in a letter to Henry Botteus[6] written in 1528, Erasmus mentions that more than half his time is devoted to reading and writing letters. Writing to Cardinal Pole,[7] Erasmus mentions the three messengers, and to Polydore Vergil[8] the four, who were waiting to be laden with his letters. Erasmus refers to the enormous number of letters he received in a letter to Bernard Boerio,[9] whilst in letters to Julius Pflug[10] and Nicolas Mallarius[11] he refers to the great number of letters he wrote; sometimes as many as sixty or ninety in a day. In the later years of his life, Erasmus wrote rough drafts of his letters which were copied out neatly by his secretaries before being sent out. Earlier he wrote his letters out himself and his secretaries copied them for preservation.[12] There was of course no postal service and letters were transmitted either by servants or friends. Erasmus complains of the consequent uncertainty of delivery in a letter to Natalis Beda:

> Egregie vir, responderam epistolae tuae, miseramque Argentoratum, ut illinc transmitteretur ad vos; sed quum nullus inveniretur

idoneus, rediit ad nos. Hunc nuncium provatim conduxi mea pecunia, qui tuas Annotationes ad me perferat.[13]

Illustrious Sir, I had replied to your letter, and sent it to Strasburg, so that it could be sent on to you from there, but since no one suitable could be found, it has come back to me. Now I have privately hired this messenger with my own money, and he can bring your comments back to me.

We learn that a letter addressed to Erasmus took well over a year to reach him,[14] whilst some letters never reached him at all.[15]

Erasmus started to write letters during his youth. He probably did not at first write them with a view to publication, but several collections of his letters were published during his own lifetime. In a letter to Beatus Rhenanus[16] which appears as a preface to a collection entitled *Epistolae ad diversos*,[17] published at Basle by Froben in 1521, Erasmus claims to have been reluctant to allow the publication of his letters, and to have allowed Beatus Rhenanus to publish a previous selection which would not offend anyone, only because his friends were so importunate, and because people who possessed copies of his letters were threatening to publish them whether Erasmus liked it or not. In a letter to John Herwagen,[18] published as the preface to a collection of Erasmus' letters printed in 1531,[19] Erasmus again states that he did not normally write his letters for publication. A further passage from his letter to Beatus Rhenanus gives important information on Erasmus' attitude to his letters:

Ego quum adolescens atque etiam aetate virili, plurimas scripserim epistolas, vix ullam tamen in hoc scripsi ut aederetur. Exercebam stilum, fallebam ocium, nugabar cum amiculis, stomacho morem gerebam; denique nihil aliud hic fere quam ludebam, nihil minus expectans quam ut huiusmodi naenias describerent et asservarent amici. Nam Senae cum essem, humanissimus ille Piso, qui tum Regis sui nomine oratorem agebat apud Iulium Pontificem, repperit apud bibliopolam quendam prostantem codicem epistolarum Erasmi, sed manu descriptum: emit ac mihi misit. In hoc tametsi erant multa quae fortasse non indigna videri poterant quae servarentur, tamen offensus casu tam inopinato, totum quantus erat, Vulcano dicavi.[20]

Although when I was a young man, and also in the age of my manhood, I wrote very many letters, yet I hardly wrote any for publication. I practised my style, I beguiled my leisure, I trifled with my friends, I gave way to my displeasure—indeed I did nothing more than amuse myself as it were, expecting nothing less than that my friends should copy out and preserve such trifles. For when I was at Siena, that most courteous Piso, who was then his king's ambassador to Pope Julius, found for sale a volume of Erasmus' letters, at a bookseller's, written in manuscript, which he bought and sent to me. Although there was much in it which might have seemed worthy of preservation, yet I was annoyed by such an unlooked-for incident and I burned the whole volume.

Erasmus goes on to relate that he found several similar collections in Germany, which he likewise burned whenever he could get hold of them. However, when he found that he was powerless to remedy the situation, he allowed the publication of some of his letters, partly so that people should cease to ply him with requests, and partly so that a correct rather than an incorrect version of the letter should be printed, and so that care should be taken to delete material which might give offence. Thus it is clear that Erasmus sometimes revised his letters for publication.[21] This impression is confirmed by a letter which Erasmus wrote to William Mount-joy[22] inviting him to send any letters he might have, for publication after revision. It seems therefore that from an early date, Erasmus' letters attracted interest, and this led to their being published, some being circulated in manuscript even before being published. Beatus Rhenanus, in a letter to Charles V, implies that Erasmus' letters had attracted attention even as early as the time when he entered the service of the Bishop of Cambrai:

> Audita Erasmi fama, Cameracensis antistes Henricus ex Bergensium Regulorum familia prognatus, iuvenem iam sacris initiatum ad se vocat. . . . Videbat enim Erasmum valere litteris, valere eloquentia, moribus ingenuis praeditum, Epistolis eleganter scriptis id docentibus.[23]

> Henry of Bergen, Bishop of Cambrai, having heard of the fame of Erasmus, called to himself the young man, who had already been ordained. . . . For he saw that, as his elegantly written letters showed, Erasmus was a person of good character, who was of some ability in learning and eloquence.

In 1505, we learn from a letter written to one of his friends, Francis Theodoric[24] that Erasmus was making an attempt to collect some of the letters which he had written more elaborately than usual. Erasmus' first published work seems to have been a letter addressed to Robert Gaguin and inserted at the end of Gaguin's history of France, which was published in 1495.[25] During the next twenty years the only letters of Erasmus to be printed were a series of prefatory and dedicatory letters to his own and other people's works. In 1515 Froben issued a small volume containing four letters of Erasmus, and from then until the end of his life, numerous collections of his letters, both authorized and unauthorized, poured from the presses.[26] But only two of the letters which Erasmus wrote before his thirtieth year were published in his lifetime.[27] After his death, authorized collections were issued by his literary executors, the last one being reprinted in 1558. Important collections of Erasmus' letters were also published long after his death in Leyden by Paul Merula in 1606; by Peter Scriverius, also in Leyden, in 1615 (three times reprinted in 1617, 1642 and 1649) and in London in 1642, possibly edited by Adrian Vlacq.[28] This was followed just over fifty years later by the collection contained in the complete Leyden edition of Erasmus' works of 1703. For a good two hundred years, then, there was a reading public in Europe for the letters of Erasmus.

The reasons for this popularity are not hard to find. In his letter to Beatus Rhenanus prefixed to the *Epistolae ad diversos* Erasmus stated his belief that letters should reflect the real life of men; treatises or declamations which were merely cast in the guise of letters did not deserve to be so called. He therefore considered that the letters of Seneca to Lucilius were not true letters, because they were wanting in feeling, and that most of the letters of Cyprian, Basil, Jerome and Augustine were books rather than letters. (On just these grounds those of Erasmus' own works which are cast into letter form, no doubt to achieve that direct and less formal mode of addressing the reader which the letter form gives, are not included among the corpus of his letters, and so works such as the *Enchiridon Militis Christiani, De Virtute Amplectanda*, and *De Ratione Studii*, all in letter form, are excluded from consideration here.) Then again, there were letters which were really short declamations, such as the letters of Phalaris, amongst others. Erasmus sets out his ideal of a genuine letter:

Verum autem illud epistolarum genus quod mores, quod fortunam, quod affectus, quod publicum simul et privatum temporis statum velut in tabula repraesentat, cuius generis fere sunt Epistolae Ciceronis ac Plinii, et inter recentiores Aeneae Pii.[29]

That true type of letter, which portrays as in a picture the manners, the fortune and the emotions of the writer, together with the public and private condition of the time—such as are most of the letters of Cicero and Pliny, and among the writers of a later date, those of Aeneas Pius.

Erasmus admits however that this kind of letter is dangerous because whether anyone is praised or blamed, someone is sure to be offended. Moreover, one-time friends often become enemies, and former foes, friends. Published comments about them can often cause embarrassment. Erasmus thought that it was safer to entrust one's correspondence to a faithful friend who would publish it after one's death as Tiro had published Cicero's. Then again, a letter is often written in the mood of the moment:

> Plerique ex una quapiam epistola totum aestimant hominis inge-
> nium, quum aliquoties scribamus uvidi, nonnunquam dormitantes,
> interim lassi, interim etiam aegroti, aut aliud agentes, nonnun-
> quam alieno stomacho, frequenter ad eius cui scribimus vel
> captum vel iudicium orationis habitum attemperantes.[30]

> Most people judge the character of a man from a single letter,
> when we sometimes write in our cups, sometimes half asleep,
> sometimes when fatigued, sometimes even when ill, or doing
> something else, or out of temper, and often adapting the tenor of
> our discourse to the understanding or judgment of the man to
> whom we are writing.

The correspondence of Erasmus does indeed display that marvellous variety and truth to life which he claims as the characteristic of a good letter. His correspondents included men of every type and degree. He praises and upbraids, argues and consoles, discusses statecraft, disputes about church affairs, and indulges his taste for literary discussion. Through his letters there emerges a picture of a true Renaissance humanist, a man of wide sympathies, deeply involved in literature and life, resolute throughout all the difficulties which beset him: bodily afflictions, despair, and world weariness. Whatever the subject of his letter, it is matched by a perfectly judged style. We have seen that Erasmus had recommended the letters of Cicero and Pliny and Aeneas Pius (Pope Pius II) as models, and in his treatise *De Conscribendis Epistolis*[31] he refers the reader constantly to examples drawn from Cicero, Pliny, and Angelo Politian. What Erasmus probably admired most about these writers is the intimate style in which their letters are written, for Erasmus thought that a letter ought to be as it were a conversation between absent friends:

> Talem oportere esse dictionem Epistolae, quales sunt amicorum
> inter ipsos confabulationes.[32]

The style of a letter should be like the conversation of friends amongst themselves.

Epistolam . . . colloquium est inter absentes.[33]

A letter . . . is a conversation between those who are parted.

Cicero was undoubtedly an important influence on Erasmus' style, but Erasmus was not an absolute Ciceronian, a slavish imitator of Cicero alone:

Ut fateor Ciceroni primam in dicendo laudem deberi, ita puto ridiculum tota vita nihil aliud agere quam ut Ciceronem unum exprimas.[34]

Although I confess that the first praise in oratory is due to Cicero, I think it quite ridiculous to do nothing else throughout the whole of one's life than imitate Cicero alone.

Again, in a letter to Francis Vergara, Erasmus voices his opposition to the absolute Ciceronians:

Apud hos prope turpius est non esse Ciceronianum quam non esse Christianum: quasi vero si Cicero nunc revivisceret, de rebus Christianis non aliter loqueretur quam aetate sua loquebatur, quum praecipua pars eloquentiae sit apposite dicere.[35]

In their opinion it is almost more disgraceful not to be a Ciceronian than not to be a Christian, as if indeed, if Cicero were now to be restored to life, he would not speak differently about Christian affairs than he used to speak in his own day, since the principal duty of eloquence is to speak appropriately.

Yet Cicero undoubtedly had an important influence on the style of Erasmus. This is shown in the use of long periodic sentences, of studied antitheses, of rhetorical questions, of asyndeton and all the numerous rhetorical tricks of which a modern reader is scarcely conscious. Erasmus was of course writing in the new 'Classical' Latin style on which the Renaissance humanists set so high a value, and no doubt we are inclined to attribute specifically to Cicero more than is directly due to him. Yet in reading Cicero we gain a strong impression of his judiciousness and detachment, through which he can as it were organize and comment upon his material, and these two qualities are present in Erasmus alongside the merely verbal similarities. Consider the controlled manner in which Erasmus writes to Jodocus Gaverius upon receipt of the news of the death of his friend John Naevius, a letter which can stand comparison with Servius Sulpicius' famous letter[36] on the death of Cicero's daughter:

61

Ioannis Naevii, communis amici, nunciata mors, quemadmodum mihi gravem moerorem attulit, ita attulit et salubrem admonitionem. Non enim possum non graviter ferre tam singularis amici iacturam, praesertim quum ipse multis nominibus esset vita longissima dignissimus. Rursum mors tam subita admonet nos omnes, ne quis in eo statu velit vivere in quo nolit mori.[37]

Just as the news of the death of our common friend John Naevius has brought to me heavy grief, so it has brought me a timely warning. I cannot fail to bear heavily the loss of such an outstanding friend, especially when he was himself on many counts most worthy of a very long life. Again, so sudden a death warns us all that none of us should live in that condition in which he is unwilling to die.

Erasmus recounts the circumstances of Naevius' death, and then recalls what manner of man he was:

Quae linguae felicitas, quam prompta, quam parata dicendi facultas, si de re seria dicendum esset! Qui lepos, quae argutia, si iocis aut salibus ludere libuisset! Tum qui morum candor! quae convictus suavitas! Quam erat amicus amico, quam arcani crediti continens, quam non sordidus![38]

What felicity of speech did he have, how ready and prepared was his power of speaking, if he had to speak on a serious matter! What charm, what acuteness did he have if it pleased him to be sportive with jokes or wit! Then what frankness of manners was his! What sweetness in his way of life! What a friend to a man he was, how retentive of a secret entrusted to him, how free from vulgarity!

Erasmus then develops the letter into a general meditation on mortality and death:

Ab omni philosophia videtur alienus, qui miserius ducit mori natum quam nasci moriturum, quum utrunque pariter secundum naturam sit hominis. Verum dictu mirum quam vulgus execretur subitam mortem, adeo ut nihil frequentius, nihil vehementius apud Deum ac divos deprecetur quam mortem subitaneam et improvisam. Subito mori piis pariter atque impiis commune est. . . . Horrendum est male mori, non subito.[39]

That man seems a stranger to all philosophy who thinks it more wretched that one who has been born should die, than that one who is destined to die should be born, since both are in accord with man's nature. Indeed, it is strange to relate how the crowd of men abhors sudden death, so that they pray to God and their gods for nothing more often and more ardently than to be spared a sudden and unexpected death. To die suddenly is a thing common to the holy and unholy alike. . . . The terrible thing is to die badly, not suddenly.

This leads Erasmus on to thoughts of the right way in which to live and die:

> Quidam illud etiam nominatim a Deo flagitant, quo genere mortis mori velint et quot menses decumbere. Quanto Christianius est nihil interim aliud curare quam ut sic instituamus vitam ne, quandocunque dies ille supremus advenerit, opprimat nos imparatos, reliqua summi numinis arbitrio relinquamus! Novit Deus quid cuique maxime expediat. Una nascendi ratio est omnibus; moriendi magna varietas. Eligat ille quodcunque voluerit. Non potest male mori qui bene vixerit.[40]

> Some people even demand of God in detail the kind of death they wish to die, and how many months to be ill. How much more Christian to care about nothing else in the meanwhile, than that we may so live our lives, that when that final day shall come, it may not overwhelm us unprepared, and to leave the rest to the judgment of God? God knows what is most appropriate for each man. There is one way of being born for all men: of dying, there is a wonderful variety. Let God choose whatever one He wishes. He who has lived well, cannot die badly.

This passage introduces a long meditation on dying, on the blessings of dying well and nobly, on whether long life is to be desired, or whether to live well is more fortunate than to live long. There follows a sad catalogue of all the acquaintances of Erasmus, men of promise and learning, whom an untimely death has borne away—Andrew Ammonius, for example:

> Et suis dotibus et omni principum applausu florentem, maximis rebus destinatum subita mors intercepit. . . . Cuius equidem decessum non possum non dolere, quoties in mentem venit quam mihi fuerit iucunda eius familiaritas.[41]

> A man flourishing both with his own talents and with all the approbation of Princes, destined for the greatest future, whom sudden death carried away. . . . I cannot help mourning his death, as often as the thought of how sweet to me his friendship was comes into my mind.

The list continues with John Sixtin, John Colet, William Grocyn, John Capnio, Christopher Longolius and many more—men of promise and talent, who died early. In spite of the constant grief these deaths cause him, Erasmus maintains a resolute attitude of mind:

Nullus autem est tantus cruciatus quem humana natura non ferat, si assueverit, praesertim si adsit fortis animus. . . . Porro, quod ad animum attinet, non solum sic cogito, mitius reddi malum si quis ferat aequo animo quod vitari nequit: verumetiam hoc Evangelicae debeo philosophiae, quod corpusculum hoc totum semel dedidi Christo, non aliter quam aegrotus ac de vita periclitans se credit medico ungenti, proluenti, secanti, urenti; persuasus quod quibuscunque modis ille tractaverit hoc animae domicilium, salutis meae causa facturus sit.[42]

There is no torment so great that human nature may not bear it, if it has grown accustomed to it, especially if the mind is resolute. . . . Indeed, as far as concerns the mind, I not only think thus, that the evil can be softened if anyone bears with a calm mind what cannot be avoided; but indeed I owe this to Christianity, that I once gave all this humble body to Christ, just as a sick man, in danger of death, entrusts himself to the doctor who annoints and washes away, who cuts out and burns, believing that in whatsoever way he deals with this tiny abode of my soul, he will do it for the sake of my salvation.

From this letter we can see that Erasmus can well portray the mood of devotional humility coupled with that of spiritual conflict for which the Latin language is so well suited. The ardour of Erasmus' feelings is perfectly conveyed. Erasmus writes other letters of consolation on the death of his friends. Amongst those worthy of note are his letter to William Budaeus[43] on the death of William of Croy, Archbishop of Toledo, his letter to Adrian Barlandus[44] on the death of Martin Dorp and his letter to John of Heemstede[45] on the death of Froben—the first two simple, restrained and resigned, the latter a long elegiac praising Froben's virtues whilst he lived, together with a moving narration of his manner of death:

Quis enim tale non amet ingenium? Solus erat amico amicus, tam simplex ac syncerus, ut etiam si quid voluisset simulare aut dissimulare, non potuisset repugnante natura; tam promptus et alacer ad bene merendum de omnibus, ut indignis etiam ex ipso beneficii quippiam accessisse gauderet.[46]

Who would not love a nature such as his? He alone was a real friend to a friend, so simple and sincere, that even if he had wished to feign or disguise anything, his nature would have rebelled, and he could not have done it: he was so ready and quick to deserve well of all, that he would rejoice that some kindliness on his part had come even to those who did not deserve it.

Ita noster Frobenius rebus humanis exemptus ad vitam transiit feliciorem, uxori, liberis, amicis acerbo luctu, toti civitati notisque omnibus gravi sui desiderio relicto. Ob huius mortem decebat omnes qui colunt bonas litteras, pullatos lachrymas et luctum sumere, apio flosculisque sepulchrum ornare, lymphas aspergere, odores adolere, si quid talibus officiis proficeretur.[47]

And so our Froben, delivered from the affairs of this earth, has passed to a happier life, leaving his wife, his children and his friends with a bitter grief, and the whole state, and all his acquaintances with a heavy longing for him. Because of his death, it behoved all who revere good letters, clad in mourning garments, to summon up tears and sorrow, and to adorn his tomb with parsley and little flowers, and to sprinkle water, and bestow sweet spices, if there were any profit in such duties.

The sentiments are conventional, and in calling upon his friends to scatter the tomb with flowers Erasmus has fallen into a theme of pastoral elegy. Yet his tribute is not glib and trite but moving and effective. We do not read Erasmus' letters primarily to seek a philosophy of life, or for spiritual consolation; and in this letter he is only expressing a common feeling of grief and sadness following the death of a friend. Yet we do not put down the letter without sharing in Erasmus' spiritual victory, and not the smallest part of the attraction of the letters is that there are some which are a spiritual autobiography as ardent as St Augustine's *Confessions*.

There are many examples of this kind of devotional prose in the letters of Erasmus, the discursive meditation on human life of a man whose faith remained steadfast. Here is Erasmus writing to Pope Adrian VI:

David sua cithara succurrebat Sauli, quoties a spiritu Domini malo agitabatur. Quod si tantam vim habet humana musica ad mutandas affectiones corporum et animorum, quanto credenda est efficatior coelestis haec ac divina musica ad purgandos animos nostros a morbis spiritualibus ac spiritibus huius seculi malis. Ingens morbus est ambitio, pessimus spiritus est livor et odium.[48]

David came to the help of Saul with his lyre, as often as he was vexed by the evil spirit from God. But if human music has so much power in changing the moods of the body and the mind, how much more is this heavenly and divine music to be thought effective in purging our minds from spiritual illnesses, and from the evil spirits of this age. Ambition is a mighty disease, envy and hatred is the most evil spirit.

In similar vein he writes to John Carondelet:

Quumque tam fugax sit vita nostra, interim ea negligimus sine quibus nulla spes est cuiquam assequendae salutis. Nisi condonaro fratri quod in me peccavit, mihi non condonabit Deus quod in ipsum admisi. Nisi mundum cor habuero, non videbo Deum. Hoc igitur totis studiis agendum erat, hoc meditandum, hoc urgendum, ut livore, ut invidia, ut odio, ut superbia, ut avaricia, ut libidine purgem animum. Non damnaberis si nescias utrum Spiritus a Patre et Filio proficiscentis unicum sit principium an duo; sed non effugies exitium, nisi curaris interim habere fructus Spiritus, qui sunt charitas, gaudium, pax, patientia, benignitas, bonitas, longanimitas, mansuetudo, fides, modestia, continentia, castitas.[49]

Since our life is so fleeting, and we meanwhile neglect those things without which no one has any hope of obtaining salvation. Unless I pardon my brother his sins against me, God will not pardon in me my sins against Him. Unless I have a pure heart, I shall not see God. This then was my task in all my studies, this was what I thought on, this was my goal, that I might purge my mind from jealousy, envy, hatred, pride, greed, and lust. You will not be damned if you do not know whether there is one origin or two to the Spirit having its origin in the Father and the Son; but you will not escape damnation if you do not take care in the meanwhile to possess the fruits of the spirit, which are charity, joy, peace, patience, kindliness, goodness, forbearance, gentleness, faith, modesty, continence, chastity.

Erasmus is not saying anything very new; but nonetheless ennobling sentiments eloquently expressed have it in them to hold our attention and interest.

Erasmus' own ideal of life was centred upon literature—'bonae literae; sine quibus quid est hominum vita?[50] (Good letters, without which what is the life of man?) A good many of his letters are about books and literature. He writes to Richard Sparcheford[51] to thank him for the gift of a syntax, and sends him a Chrysostom in return, wondering which of them will profit the more by the other's gift. He writes to Germanus Brixius:

O te terque quaterque felicem, Brixi charissime, qui te semper intra Musarum septa continueris, nec unquam attigeris spineta theologorum.[52]

O thrice and four times blessed are you, my dearest Brixius, who have always kept yourself within the enclosures of the Muses, and have never touched the thorn-hedges of the Theologians.

This suggests that his own ideal way of life was very close to the Classical ideal of *otium*, a life of urbane cultivated ease in which humane letters figured prominently. He writes longingly to Thomas Lupset:

> O te felicem, cui datum sit omnium rerum securo in Musarum viretis ludere![53]
>
> O how happy you are, to whom it has been given to sport on the greensward of the Muses, free of the care of all things!

In a letter to the printer Francis Minutius, Erasmus expresses the delight which he obtains from the style of Jacopo Sadoleto:

> Sadoleti libellum in deliciis habeo; verum illius aureum dictionis flumen consyderans, video quam meus rivus sit et turbidus et exilis. Posthac ad hoc exemplar, meum quoque stilum conabor attemperare.[54]
>
> The little book of Sadoleto is my favourite; indeed, considering the golden river of his style, I see how my own stream is both meagre and disordered. From now onwards, I shall try to accommodate my style to this pattern.

In a letter to a friend, Erasmus describes the delight which he obtains from books. He can enter into conversation with them away from the crowd, he can listen to them talking to him, but they speak only when he wishes them to; they advise him in prosperity, and console him in affliction, and they endure until the last moments of death:

> Cum his amiculis, optime N, sepultus delitesco. Quas ego tandem opes aut quae sceptra cum hac desidia commutavero?[55]
>
> With these little friends, my dearest N, I hide myself away, buried in seclusion. For what riches or what sceptres would I exchange this tranquillity?

Erasmus' views on the nobleness of literature and literary study receive their fullest expression in a letter written as a preface to an edition of Pliny's *Natural History* addressed to Stanislaus Turzo.[56] Erasmus starts by saying that magnificent buildings not only ennoble those by whose expense they were erected, and those to whom they were dedicated, but also all those who contributed to building them. He praises the famous buildings which have earned fame for their creators: the temple of Solomon, the Pyramids, the Labyrinth. Yet the builders of bridges and aqueducts, baths and harbours, deserve more praise, because they combine usefulness with magnificence. But compared to all those, what can be said about the 'living and breathing monument of his talent which Pliny has left us?'

Imo non opus est, sed thesaurus, sed vere mundus rerum omnium cognitu dignarum. Proinde non mirum si unum tot viros nobili-tavit, hodieque nobilitat. Nemo fuit tam obscurus, quin illustris esse coeperit, posteaquam huic operi manum admovit.

Perierat nobis hoc divinum munus, ni certatim a summis ingeniis advigilatum esset, ut ex ruinis pene deploratis orbi renasceretur.[57]

Indeed, it is not a work, but a treasury, indeed a world of all things worthy of being known. And so it is not to be wondered at if it alone has ennobled so many men, and today ennobles them. No one was so obscure, but that he began to be illustrious after he had put his hand to this work.

This divine work would have perished from our knowledge, had it not been eagerly watched over by the greatest talents, so that it might come forth again for this world out of ruins almost regarded as lost.

Erasmus then pays tribute to all the people who have helped to restore the text of Pliny, who is 'omnibus omnium sculptorum ac pictorum operibus anteponendum'.[58] (To be placed before all the works of all painters and sculptors.) Such was the primacy which Erasmus accorded to literary art.

But Erasmus did not devote all his time to the enjoyment of literature remote from the affairs of the world. He led an active life, and travelled all over Europe. He was an excellent storyteller, and his letters record the experiences of his journeys. Erasmus describes one such journey in a letter to James Batt:[59] how he had hired two horses at Amiens on his journey to Paris, and how it was very soon clear that the horse dealer and his apprentice were bent on robbing Erasmus and his travelling companion; Erasmus tried at first to barricade himself in the bedroom of an inn where they were staying and when that plan failed, he and his companion were forced to stay awake all night on guard. Eventually they gave the two thieves the slip, and made their way to Paris by themselves, but not before being cheated by the inn-keeper, who over-charged them and quibbled over the coins with which Erasmus wished to settle the account. Erasmus amusingly recounts how he managed to confute the inn-keeper by secretly purloining the false weight with which he was weighing the gold. These glimpses of Erasmus' tribulations and adventures have a fascination for us today. Con-sider his account of an explosion at Basle when he was in that city in 1526.[60] Erasmus had been walking leisurely in Froben's garden, induced to do so by the pleasantness of the day, and had then settled down to translate some Chrysostom, when three flashes of lightning attracted his attention. He looked up at the sky in amazement, to see whether a storm was threatening, but it was quite clear. Then he heard a loud noise, saw another flash, and then heard a bang which so frightened him that he ran back to join his companion. Erasmus then notices a sinister cloud:

> Ad laevam erat serenitas, ad dexteram conspicio novam nubis speciem, velut e terra sese proferentis in sublime, colore prope-modum cinericio, cuius cacumen velut inflexum sese demittebat. Dixisses scopulum quempiam esse, vertice nutantem in mare. Quo contemplor attentius, hoc minus videbatur nubi similis.[61]

> On the left, the sky was clear; on the right, I behold a new kind of cloud, raising itself aloft from the earth into the heavens, as it were, with an almost ashen colour, the summit of which bent itself downwards as if bowing. You would have said it was a cliff, nodding at the top towards the sea. The more attentively I looked at it, the less it seemed like a cloud.

The cause of the incident is soon made known: barrels of gun-powder had been stored in one of the towers in the city walls; a flash of lightning had entered through the chinks and set it off. The tower had been blown up, and the flying fragments had killed and injured many people, including some working in the fields outside. Erasmus is led to deplore the invention of gunpowder:

> Quis hoc machinarum genus excogitavit? Olim artes ad humanae vitae usum repertas diis attribuit antiquitas. ... Huius inventi laudem non puto cuiquam deberi, nisi vehementer ingenioso cuipiam, nec minus scelerato cacodaemoni.[62]

> Who devised an invention of this kind? In ancient times, men attributed to the gods the arts discovered for the advantage of human life. ... I do not belief that any praise for this invention is due to anyone, except to a fiend excessively ingenious, and no less wicked.

Erasmus wrote so many letters, so various in subject and mood and style, letters of commendation, consolation, and advice, for-mal letters to state leaders, informal letters to his friends, business letters, polemical letters, and many others, that one could easily fill a whole volume with examples of each. The best way to an understanding of the range and diversity of sixteenth-century letter writing is, I believe, through an examination of Erasmus' own treatise on letter writing, the *De Conscribendis Epistolis*,[63] in which the theory and practice of letter writing are discussed with great thoroughness. Handbooks on letter writing which taught the art of composing letters and documents, had existed in the Middle Ages. They were an application to letter writing of the ancient system of rhetoric. Handbooks on letter writing, much more comprehensive and elaborate, were also produced in the Renaissance. Erasmus' excuse for adding to the large number of existing handbooks was that there was not one of them which he had not found wanting in some way or other.[64] Erasmus had started to write this treatise in 1497 for the benefit of his pupils, but he did not complete it. A pirated edition was published at Cambridge in 1521. A revised edition was then published with Erasmus' sanction in 1522 at Strasburg.[65]

Erasmus opens his treatise with a plea that the subject matter of letters should be various, and that the style should be as diverse as the subject matter, and should be in accord with it:

> Nullum fere argumenti genus non recipiat Epistola: et nusquam oporteat orationis habitum cum argumenti genere dissidere.[66]

> There is almost no kind of theme which a letter may not treat, and it is never right that the style of the discourse should be at variance with the type of theme.

Erasmus defends the artificial letter against those who prefer that a letter should be unstudied. He had 'rather that a letter should smell of the lamp, than of liquor, of the ointment box, and of the goat'.[67] He discusses at some length the occasions when a letter may be serious or even tragic in tone, to what extent its diction should be clear, and whether it may include unusual words.[68] Erasmus then sets out his ideas of what a letter ought to be:

> Itidem et ego eam Epistolam optimam iudico, quae a vulgato hoc et indocto literarum genere quam longissime recedat: quae sententiis exquisitissimis, verbis electissimis, sed aptis constet: quae argumento, loco, tempori, personae, quam maxime sit accommodata, quae amplissimis de rebus agens, sit gravissima: de mediocribus, concinna: de humilibus, elegans, et faceta: in iocis acumine delectet ac lepore, in encomiis apparatu: in exhortando vehemens sit, et animosa: in consolando blanda sit, et amica: in suadendo, gravis sit et sententiosa: in narrando, lucida et graphica: in petendo, verecunda: in commendando, officiosa; in rebus secundis, gratulabunda: in afflictis, seria.[69]

> In like manner I too consider that that letter is best which is as far removed as possible from the common and unlearned type of letter; which stands out with the nicest opinions, and the choicest words, but ones that are apt; which is as closely suited as possible to the argument, place, time, addressee; which when dealing with

weighty matters is serious, which with mediocre matters is neat; with humble matters elegant and witty; which in jokes delights by its acuteness and charm, in praise by its pomp; which is ardent and spirited in exhortation, soothing and friendly in consolation; which is serious and sententious in advising; modest in requests; in narrating, clear and graphic; in commending, dutiful; in time of happiness, congratulatory; in times of distress, grave.

In short, a letter should be versatile, and appropriate to its subject. He reiterates the view expressed in his letter to Beatus Rhenanus that the name 'letter' might well be denied to the kind written as an exercise, or for the display of talent (such as the letters of Phalaris and Ovid's *Heroides*); to those that are books rather than letters, such as most of those of Jerome, Cyprian and Augustine; and to those that are rather speeches, and are written at length to princes and magistrates on difficult and complicated subjects.[70] The true letter is as it were the conversation of friends between themselves, containing simplicity, candour, pleasantry and wit.[71] Erasmus continues with chapters discussing the instruction of children in the arts of writing.[72] He then discusses one or two technical matters, including the form of greeting, the use of the formula 'S.D.', the use of cognomina in forms of address, the absurdity of piling up a long series of titles in the salutation, the appropriate adjectives which are used to designate the various civil and ecclesiastical dignitaries, e.g., 'Consul vigilantissime', 'Senator splendidissime', 'Archiepiscopi reverendissime', etc.[73] He discusses how to ask a friend to convey greetings to someone else, and how to reply to such a greeting, how to say farewell, and how to date a letter.[74] In Chapter XXIX of his treatise, Erasmus discusses the arrangement of material, and how to pass easily from one part of a letter to another by the use of such phrases as: 'Sed tristia mittamus, revertamur ad laetiora.' (Let us lay aside these sad events and return to happier ones.) Or 'Vulnus aperui, nunc remedium ostendam.'[75] (I have opened the wound, now I will show you the remedy.) Erasmus then illustrates these transitions by means of a model letter[76] which he has written from one Domitius to his friend Lucius, a letter which has many sections, including lamentation on a friend's death, the thanks given to Lucius for passing on some kind remarks made to him about Domitius, congratulations to Lucius on the birth of his nephew warnings, advice, exhortations, and news of Domitius' private affairs. There are several model letters of this sort in the *De*

Conscribendis Epistolis, and they have an interest in that they show that Erasmus was able to compose an artificial letter according to a formula, expressing all the feigned emotions in accordance with the terms of the formula.

In Chapters XXXI–XXXII Erasmus comes to the central tenet of his discussion.[77] He applies the antique theory of oratory to the writing of letters. He proposes not to divide letters into types according to subject matter, since otherwise there would be an infinite number of categories of letter, letters in which the writer rejoiced, feared, grieved, hoped, was angry or flattered, hated or loved, and so on. Instead, Erasmus links the types of letters with the antique classification of rhetoric into the deliberative, epideictic, and judicial types. Deliberative letters would be letters of conciliation and reconciliation; exhortation and dissuasion; advice about anything, letters of consolation, petition, commendation, warning and of love. To the epideictic genre belong descriptions of persons, regions, estates, citadels, fountains, gardens, mountains, marvellous events, storms, journeys, banquets, entertainments, buildings and processions. To the judicial type belong letters of accusation, complaint, defence, expostulation, vindication, reproach, letters which threaten, and letters of abuse and deprecation. To these three classes, Erasmus adds another, the familiar letter. Here belong the news letter, in which distant friends are informed of the writer's personal news; the letter of announcement, which gives information on new developments either in public, private, or even domestic affairs; the letter of congratulation; the letter of lament, deploring the fortunes of the writer or of someone else; the business letter, in which some personal business is entrusted to someone else to be carried out; the letter of thanks for service done; the letter of commendation, giving praise to a servant for doing his duty; the dutiful letter, which of its own accord offers help and goodwill to a friend; and the jocose letter, which delights the mind by its sportive urbanity. On top of this, there are the letters which deal with questions of dispute, enquiry, and theory, together with letters concerned with theology and ethics. Erasmus defends his system of classifying letters by the mode of argument, as opposed to the Greek system of classifying by the person to whom the letter is addressed, pointing out that what the Greeks describe as a letter to a friend, could be a letter of love, expostulation, advice, or rebuke etc.

Erasmus then gives detailed advice on how to begin a letter,[78] whether a direct opening is permissible, and how the opening of a letter differs from the opening of a speech. He then discusses the *Captatio Benevolentiae*—the method of placing the person addressed in a favourable frame of mind. One could say that the parents of the writer and addressee were friends, and the writer had grown to love the addressee from earliest childhood, or one could exaggerate the great kindness of the person addressed, or praise his virtue and erudition, or relate the writer's own misfortunes in order to arouse pity, or relate what he had suffered at the hands of a common enemy. A good example of a *Captatio Benevolentiae* is that which opens Erasmus' letter to Sigismund, king of Poland,[79] in which Erasmus first relates all the reasons which nearly deterred him from writing: it was immodest for a man so humble to address one so exalted; Sigismund would be too occupied with mighty affairs of state to be able to spare time to read Erasmus' letter, but nonetheless, Sigismund's outstanding goodness of nature, and Erasmus' zeal towards him, and his admiration of his virtues dispelled all his qualms; and so he continues with a series of courtly compliments.

In great detail, Erasmus next discussed the letter of exhortation,[80] which is a subdivision of the deliberative class of letter—how to spur someone to achievement by praise, by saying that the achievement would be pious, magnificent, glorious, remarkable, new, difficult, or thus far unattempted. In similar fashion, Erasmus then teaches how to write a letter of exhortation by appealing to the feeling of hope, fear, love, hatred, compassion, desire to excel, to the expectations of friends and enemies; he deals with the use of rhetorical *exempla*, teaches how to reach the peroration, how to modify the exhortation, and what style is the appropriate one. He then discusses rhetorical *amplificatio*,[81] but he does not dwell on the subject, for as he reminds his readers:

> Rhetoricen hic non docemus, sed indicamus duntaxat, quod ad scribendas epistolas attinet.[82]

> We are not teaching here the Art of Rhetoric, but only indicating what parts of it pertain to letter writing.

Erasmus then provides a model of an exhortatory letter, from an uncle to a nephew,[83] exalting the nephew's achievements, praising him because of the things he has done well, exhorting him through his family, his father, his nature, his learning, through hope and fear, through *exempla* drawn from various periods of history, both Greek and Roman, from the Bible, and from his ancestors. In like manner, Erasmus gives advice on dissuasion, and then deals in the same way with another branch of the deliberative class of letter writing, the letter of persuasion, which embraces letters of petition, commendation, advice and warning and which Erasmus admits is not very different from the letter of exhortation. 'Iam ad suasorium genus veniamus: quod quidem ab illo superiori (i.e., the exhortatory type) non admodum abhorret.'[84] Erasmus had earlier admitted that the two types of letter were very similar, and explained the difference as follows:

> Suasio probationibus docet: exhortatio stimulis exstimulat. Suasor sententiam mutat: exhortator animum addit.[85]

> Persuasion teaches by proof, exhortation arouses with spurs. The persuader changes opinions; the exhorter adds spirit.

Erasmus then discusses tricks of logic, such as how to make two alternatives appear mutually exclusive[86] and he continues by discussing the working out of various themes, such as for example, the theme that it is the part of a wise man to have regard for his reputation far more diligently than for his wealth, quite as much as for life itself.[87] This is the kind of argument which can easily be inserted into a letter. Erasmus then gives an example of a letter of persuasion, in which a man whose mother has died, and whose sister has taken the veil, is urged to marry.[88]

Still within the deliberative class of letter, Erasmus discusses the letter of consolation, and sets out the reasons with which a man may be consoled.[89] One can say that there is no reason for grief, since nothing sad can happen to a wise man except disgrace, and that no one can be harmed save by himself. Or the writer can deny that he is writing a letter of consolation, and say that he does not doubt, since he has had many examples of the addressee's outstanding wisdom, that the unbroken greatness of his mind is greater than all the storms of fortune; or the writer can play down the evil, and magnify the good results which may well come from it. Or he can endeavour to demonstrate that what has happened is not an evil, or that it is not so serious as it seems, since there is no evil from which some good may not be extracted. Erasmus elaborates all these points and sets out an example.[90] A friend is consoling Canidius, a man distinguished in the service of his country, exiled to distant parts because of the envy of political opponents, having left his wife and little children behind. Erasmus then adds a series of consolatory phrases drawn from the letters of Cicero and Pliny, together with some of his own invention, plus a few phrases which can be inserted into letters replying to letters of consolation.

Erasmus next discusses the letter of petition:[91] how to ask for something either directly or indirectly, depending on the nature of the request: how to exaggerate one's own need, how to stress the generosity of the addressee, how to admit the consciousness of one's own immodesty, how to ask for money, how to make a request when the writer has behaved badly. Here Erasmus adds two fictitious letters as models. The first presents a young man who had lost all his money at dice, and had an affair with his mother's maid, whom he has promised to marry.[92] His father has disowned him, and so he writes to a friend of his father's asking him to intercede. The second is a letter written to a bishop asking him to use his influence to procure the writer an official appointment.[93] Once again Erasmus refers the reader to the letters of Cicero and Pliny for examples of phrases which can be used in letters of petition. He then continues by discussing at length letters of commendation, admonition, and even love letters.[94]

Erasmus then turns his attention to the second main class of letters, the epideictic class,[95] which frequently overlaps with the deliberative class, as, for example, when praise of a person occurs in a letter of commendation or consolation, or when a description of a city is found in a letter urging someone to change his residence. Erasmus succinctly summarizes what things ought to be mentioned in the descriptions of people, places, buildings, rivers, lakes, fields and mountains. But he does not dwell on the subject since it is dealt with sufficiently by the rhetoricians.[96]

Finally he deals with the judicial branch of letter writing,[97] which consists mainly of letters of accusation and complaint. Once more, the precepts of the orators on judicial eloquence can be applied to letter writing. Erasmus gives an example[98] of a letter of this kind, a letter written to ask for justice against a guest who has seduced his host's maid and eloped with his daughter. In this class Erasmus includes letters of expostulation,[99] for example, letters complaining that no reply has been received to one's letters, or that a friend has been too remiss in looking after the writer's interests. He discusses too the letter of justification,[100] in which the writer defends himself against the charges that have been made, the letter of reproach,[101] the abusive letter,[102] and the letter of apology.[103] Finally he deals with the remaining types of letter,[104] the news letter, the business letter, the *Actio Gratiarum* in which thanks are returned for benefits rendered, the letter of lamentation in which the writer pours out his own troubles on to the bosom of a friend (which is allied to the letter of consolation), the letter of congratulation, the letter in which one introduces oneself to someone with whom it is desired to start a correspondence, as when one learned man writes to another in a spirit of literary companionship, the letter voluntarily offering help to a friend, and the letter of disputation or enquiry between the erudite upon some learned matter or other. There the treatise abruptly ends.

No doubt some of the distinctions between the various types of letter are over-precise, but nonetheless it does illustrate not only the formulaic nature, but also the complexity and range of letter writing during the Renaissance, not least in the letters of Erasmus himself, a complexity and range which establishes him as one of the great writers of Latin letters. The treatise also shows that letter writing was a conscious branch of literary art. It can with more truth be said of the letters of Erasmus, what Erasmus once said of the letters of his friend Marian Accard:

> Binis litteris tuis ... mihi immortalitatis (munus) infundis. Nam si scripta tua, quae mortem nesciunt, mei meminerint, quis de nominis mei immortalitate dubitabit?[105]

> In your two letters ... you present to me the gift of immortality. For if your writings, which know not death, remember me, who will doubt the immortality of my name?

So high was the value which Erasmus himself set upon letters.

NOTES

[1] *Ad Familiares*, vii. 22.

[2] *Ad Atticum*, v. 1.

[3] John Le Clerc (ed.), *Desiderii Erasmi Roterodami Opera Omnia*, 10 vols., Leyden, 1703–6—hereafter cited as *Opera Omnia*. All my quotations from Erasmus are from this edition, except for quotations from his letters, which are from the edition of P. S. Allen (12 vols., Oxford 1906–58).

[4] Allen, *Erasmi Epistolae*.

[5] 'Catalogus Lucubrationum', *Opera Omnia*, I. sig. ******1 recto.

[6] 'Nunc plusquam dimidium temporis datur legendis ac scribendis epistolis. Allen, *op. cit.*, VII. 376 (1985).

[7] 'Dulcissimum esset diutius per litteras tecum confabulari, ni mihi nunc eodem die onerandi fuissent tres baiuli; quorum unus adit Galliam, alter Brabantiam, tertius hic est Carolus meus.' *Ibid.*, VI. 192 (1627).

[8] 'Eruditissime Polydore, decreveram tecum prolixis epistolis confabulari; sed incommode incidit ut mihi praeter Livinum eodem tempore quatuor baiuli forent epistolis onerandi.' *Ibid.*, V. 542 (1494).

[9] 'Si quid omnino mihi credis, hoc tibi persuadeas velim, Bernarde suavissime, quum ex omnibus mundi plagis fasciculatim adferantur litterae, multis retro mensibus nullas venisse tuis gratiores.' *Ibid.*, IX. 253 (2481).

[10] 'Eodem tempore plures sexaginta scribende sunt epistole, et in his aliquot, quae iusti prope voluminis instar habent.' *Ibid.*, IX. 186 (2451).

[11] 'Ut eodem tempore scriberem epistolas p.m. nonaginta, quarum aliquot sunt hac duabus paginis longiores.' *Ibid.*, IX. 230 (2466).

[12] *Ibid.*, III. 632.

[13] *Ibid.*, VI. 147 (1596).

[14] 'Scito tuam epistolam prolixam mense Septembri, anno 1526 scriptam ... mihi redditam esse.' Erasmus' letter was written in March 1528. *Ibid.*, VII. 358 (1971).

[15] 'Significas te quater ad me scripsisse. Primam et ultimam epistolam accepi, duae mediae redditae non sunt: quare noli scribere nisi per certissimos nuncios.' *Ibid.*, V. 569 (1510).

[16] *Ibid.*, IV. 499 (1206).

[17] *Epistolae D. Erasmi Roterodami ad diversos et aliquot ad illum per amicos eruditos ex ingentibus fasciculis schedarum collectae*, Basle, 1521.

[18] 'Ut ex immenso epistolarum acervo flosculis notarem quas expediret excudi, quanquam vix ullas in hoc scribere soleo.' Allen, *op. cit.*, IX. 314 (2518).

[19] *Des. Erasmi Roterodami, Epistolarum Floridarum liber unus, antehac nunquam excussus*, Basle, 1531.

[20] Allen, *op. cit.*, IV. 499 (1206).

[21] See Allen, *op. cit.*, III. 7n., for his remarks on a letter known to have been revised for publication.

[22] 'Non edam nisi commutatis que erunt commutanda.' *Ibid.*, III. 236 (783).

[23] In prefatory material to *Opera Omnia*, I. sig ***1 recto.

[24] 'Vehementer mihi gratum feceris, amice iucundissime, si dederis operam ut epistolae, quas accuratius ad alios atque alios scripsi, quantum potest colligantur.' Allen, *op. cit.*, I. 415 (186).

[25] Robert Gaguin, *De origine et gestis Francorum Compendium*, Paris, 1495. Allen, *op. cit.*, I. 148 (45).

[26] Francis Morgan Nichols, *The Epistles of Erasmus from his earliest letters to his fifty-first year*, London, 1901, pp. xxvi-lvii, gives a thorough account of the printed editions of Erasmus' letters.

[27] Nichols, *op. cit.*, p. xxii.

[28] Nichols, *op. cit.*, pp. xlv–liv.

[29] Allen, *op. cit.*, IV. 501 (1206).

[30] *Ibid.*

[31] *Opera Omnia*, 'De Conscribendis Epistolis', I. cols 341–484.

[32] *Ibid.*, col. 350 C.

[33] *Ibid.*, col. 367 E.

[34] Allen, *op. cit.*, VI. 345 (1713).

[35] *Ibid.*, VII. 194 (1885).

[36] *Ad Familiares*, iv. 5.

[37] Allen, *op. cit.*, V. 238 (1347).

[38] *Ibid.*

[39] *Ibid.*, V. 239–40 (1347).

[40] *Ibid.*, V. 240 (1347).

[41] *Ibid.*, V. 247 (1347).

[42] *Ibid.*, V. 248–9 (1347).

[43] *Ibid.*, IV. 442 (1184).

[44] *Ibid.*, VI. 111 (1584).

[45] *Ibid.*, VII. 225 (1900).

[46] *Ibid.*, VII. 226 (1900).

[47] *Ibid.*, VII. 228 (1900).

[48] *Ibid.*, V. 108 (1304).

[49] *Ibid.*, V. 177 (1334).

[50] *Ibid.*, VII. 360 (1973).

[51] *Ibid.*, VII. 153 (1867).

[52] *Ibid.*, VI. 148 (1597).

[53] *Ibid.*, VI. 187 (1624).

[54] *Ibid.*, VI. 158 (1604).

[55] *Ibid.*, I. 289 (125).

[56] *Ibid.*, VI. 16 (1544).

[57] *Ibid.*, VI. 18 (1544).

[58] *Ibid.*, VI. 19 (1544).

[59] *Ibid.*, I. 275 (119).

[60] *Ibid.*, VI. 417 (1756).

[61] *Ibid.*, VI. 418 (1756).

[62] *Ibid.*, VI. 419–20 (1756).

[63] *v.* note 31.

[64] Allen, *op. cit.*, I. 198 (71).

[65] Nichols, *op. cit.*, pp. 129, 165.

[66] *Opera Omnia*, 'De Conscribendis Epistolis', I. col. 345 B.

[67] *Ibid.*, col. 346 D.

[68] *Ibid.*, cols 347–9.

[69] *Ibid.*, col. 349 C–D.

[70] *Ibid.*, col. 350 B–C.

[71] *Ibid.*, col. 350 C–D.

[72] *Ibid.*, cols 351–64.

[73] *Ibid.*, cols 364–72.

[74] *Ibid.*, cols 372–6.

[75] *Ibid.*, cols 376–7.

[76] *Ibid.*, cols 377–9.

[77] *Ibid.*, cols 379–81.
[78] *Ibid.*, col. 381.
[79] Allen, *op. cit.*, VII. 59 (1819).
[80] *Opera Omnia*, 'De Conscribendis Epistolis', I. cols 385–91.
[81] *Ibid.*, col. 392.
[82] *Ibid.*, col. 394 A.
[83] *Ibid.*, cols 394–6.
[84] *Ibid.*, col. 402 A.
[85] *Ibid.*, col. 381 C.
[86] *Ibid.*, col. 403.
[87] *Ibid.*, col. 407.
[88] *Ibid.*, cols 414–24.
[89] *Ibid.*, col. 426.
[90] *Ibid.*, cols 427–30.
[91] *Ibid.*, col. 435.
[92] *Ibid.*, col. 436 C.
[93] *Ibid.*, col. 436 F.
[94] *Ibid.*, cols 440–54.
[95] *Ibid.*, col. 454.
[96] 'Quod satis luculenter a Rhetoribus praeceptum . . . prudens praetereo.'
Ibid., col 455 A.
[97] *Ibid.*, col. 455.
[98] *Ibid.*, col. 456.
[99] *Ibid.*, col. 457 E.
[100] *Ibid.*, col. 459.
[101] *Ibid.*, col. 462.
[102] *Ibid.*, col. 464.
[103] *Ibid.*
[104] *Ibid.*, cols 466–84.
[105] Allen, *op. cit.*, II. 524–5 (564).

IV

Erasmus: Biblical Scholar and Reformer

B. HALL

MARK PATTISON wrote that Erasmus 'in whom the Humanist and Reformer were pretty equally mixed perceived what a powerful weapon the Greek original [of the New Testament] might be made'.[1] In fact this was to be the chief of several powerful weapons which Erasmus used to advance his programme of religious reform. The theme of the Erasmian humanistic reform was summed up in his own phrase *philosophia Christi*. Here we are shown the centrality of Christ found through the Bible, especially the Gospels, without reference to the dogmatic definitions of scholasticism or to many of the popular forms of piety which had developed in Catholicism, to both of which, Erasmus claimed, the learning and piety of the age of the Fathers of the first centuries of the Church were to be preferred. The anti-dogmatic, anti-speculative and anti-scholastic attitude of Erasmus led him to insist on that simplicity of faith in Christ which he proclaimed and supported with eloquent latinity, characteristic of the Erasmian movement of religious reform. This movement was a powerful influence on the many Catholics (as well as on many of those who were to become Protestants) concerned about the moral, social and religious problems of the time who recognized the need for a new moral and intellectual motivation to bring improvement. Sir Thomas More wrote to Erasmus in December 1516 nearly nine months after the publication of Erasmus' Greek and Latin New Testament: 'The Bishop of Winchester, who is, as you are aware, a man of very sound judgement, was present at a large gathering of distinguished people when the conversation turned upon you and your lucubrations; he testified, to everyone's approval, that your

version of the New Testament was better to him than ten commentaries, since it brought so much light to bear upon it.'² This
Bishop of Winchester was Richard Foxe who in the following
year was to found Corpus Christi College, Oxford, where he
wished to promote those new studies which Erasmus had so
strongly emphasized, at the same time as Erasmus himself was
preparing the way for the founding of the Trilingual College at
Louvain which he hoped would become the international centre of
this renewal.

There can be no doubt that the inspiration of this trilingual
'new learning' lay in the work of that saint whom Erasmus most
admired, Jerome, who had been *Hebraeus, Graecus, Latinis trilinguis*,
with all that this implied: and the influence of Jerome on Erasmus
was fundamental since he adopted something of Jerome's style
and more of his methods as a scholar. From his youth in the
monastery at Steyn to his closing years in the new world of the
transformed *Respublica Litterarum* which he had helped to create,
Erasmus was never to be far from Jerome. Jerome has recorded
that he had known a deep struggle between his love for the pagan
classical writers and his love for the Scriptures: for Erasmus these
were not so much opposed as transmuted. Towards the end of his
career in his *Ciceronianus* he challenged the pedantic Ciceronianism
of some humanists, showing it to be a lifeless antiquarianism, and
affirmed yet once again the importance of the intimate association
of the best in Classical culture with Christian values.

> BULEPHORUS: He who will bring to the study of Christian philo-
> sophy the zeal which Cicero brought to that of profane philo-
> sophy; he who will draw into himself the Psalms and the
> Prophets as Cicero did with the pagan poets; he who will employ
> his nights in learning the decrees of Apostles, the rites of the
> Church, the birth, the progress and the fall of the Christian
> republic, as Cicero searched the institutions and the laws of
> Roman provinces, municipalities and of allied nations; and
> through all these studies has prepared himself for the present
> time—that man will have the right to pretend to the name of
> Ciceronian.
> NOSOPONUS: But all the studies which you have enumerated will
> make us speak as Christians not as Ciceronians.
> BULEPHORUS: What then? . . .³

Here Erasmus demonstrates the need for what he called a 'Christian philosophy' which would gradually transform the life of the

contemporary Church and society through the study of the Bible, the Church Fathers, and Christian origins, and through taking warning from the Church's past weaknesses—for Erasmus, major weaknesses lay in much of the thought and many of the practices of the later medieval Church. It is characteristic of Erasmus, though he had begun his ecclesiastical career as an Augustinian canon, that he chose Jerome from his early days as the symbol of this renewal, and not Augustine, since Augustine was so much the master of the medieval mind. To appeal to Jerome however was to go back to what he conceived to be a golden age, the first Christian centuries which lay behind the middle ages, since the latter was the period when, for Erasmus, the 'barbarians' (that is, the scholastic theologians) triumphed.

When Erasmus began his lifelong and increasing devotion to Jerome is not easily determined, but the influence of the Brethren of the Common Life on his youth was more marked than he was afterwards ready to admit. The house of the Brethren at Deventer where he had studied was dedicated to Jerome; and from among the earlier of his surviving letters we know of his friendship with the Augustinian canon Cornelius Gerard, probably his teacher, who was made laureate by the Emperor Maximilian (this at least suggests that he was a skilful latinist), and who in 1516 was known to be working on a life of Jerome based on preparatory studies he had made while he was at the University of Paris in 1497. While still in the convent at Steyn, Erasmus wrote to Gerard in 1489 with approval of Jerome. He also told Gerard that he had copied out all the letters of Jerome and found in them weapons against 'the barbarians', and that from these letters he had learned that ignorant barbarism (*rusticitatem*) is not holiness, and sound latinity (*disertitudinem*) is not identical with impiety.[4] It is certain that by 1500 he had committed himself to editing the works of Jerome for he wrote in December of that year to another correspondent, Greverade:

> My mind has long burned with incredible ardour to illustrate with a commentary the letters of Jerome. In daring to conceive so great a design which no one has hitherto attempted, I feel that some god inflames and directs my heart. I am moved by the piety of that heavenly man of all Christians beyond question the most learned and most eloquent; whose writings though they deserve to be read and learned everywhere and by all, are read by few, admired by fewer still, and understood by scarcely any. . . . What a task it will

be in the first place to clear away the errors which during so many
ages have become established in the text. . . . What a style, what a
mastery of language. . . .[5]

And to James Batt he wrote in the same month that he wished 'to
restore the whole work of Jerome greatly as it is corrupted,
mutilated and confused by the ignorance of the theologians'.[6] It
was from Jerome that Erasmus learned that he could live a life of
usefulness and honour in combining the best of literary culture
with Christian piety. It was from Jerome that he first evolved the
philosophia Christi with which he opposed both the logic of the
scholastic theologians and certain debased forms of popular piety.
For Erasmus, Jerome was the ideal of the true theologian unlike
Augustine who had disturbed the simplicity of the Gospels and
Epistles of the first days of the Church with his philosophic
subtleties on sin and grace. In the preface to volume II of the
edition of Jerome's works in which he shared as editor he stated
plainly that Jerome is the best of theologians, and not even the
Greek Fathers produced a better. 'Jerome is a river of gold, he
who has Jerome alone needs no more ample library.' He was to
echo again in 1515 what he had written to Greverade in 1500,
'The work of correcting and commenting on Jerome interests my
mind so warmly, that I feel as if I had been inspired by some
god.'[7]

There was, however, another major influence on the young
Erasmus, which would continue with him for some time and one
which led him to produce that work, his edition of the Greek New
Testament with Latin translation and notes, which was to prove to
be so revolutionary. At eighteen Erasmus had already epitomized
the *Elegantiae* of Lorenzo Valla and from that time his mind was
gripped by the brilliance of style, the subtle and attractive latinity
which clothed the writings of Valla, who grounded them on an
erudition applied to their content with cool realism and clear
judgment. In 1489 he wrote to Cornelius Gerard defending Valla,
saying that the greatest praise is due to Valla who had 'with great
industry, zeal and labour repelled the absurdities of the barbarians,
rescued buried literature from destruction and restored to Italy the
splendour of her former eloquence'.[8] He found another side to
Valla's work when he discovered, in the summer of 1504, in the
library of the Premonstratensian Abbey of Parc at Louvain, a
manuscript of Valla's annotations on the Greek New Testament,

which showed Erasmus what possibilities lay in Valla's grammatical exegesis: here too he saw no doubt the practical application of
part of Jerome's methods in handling Scripture.

From now on Erasmus was determined to work on the Greek
New Testament at the same time as his labours on Jerome. He
foresaw trouble in going directly to the Greek and leaving aside
the Vulgate version, and probably one reason for his publishing
Valla's annotations was to prepare the way for his own fuller and
more revolutionary work. His preface to Valla's book, published
in 1505, was addressed to an Englishman Christopher Fisher,
papal protonotary in Paris. Here he asks,

> What crime is it in Laurentius if after collating some ancient and
> correct Greek copies he has noted in the New Testament, which
> is derived from the Greek, some passages which either differ from
> our version or seem to be inaptly rendered owing to a passing want
> of vigilance in the translator, or are expressed more significantly
> in the Greek; or, finally, if it appears that something in our text is
> corrupt?[9]

Typically he cites Jerome's authority for understanding and
translating 'by erudition and command of language'. And how
ominous to traditional theologians would be the proud claim of
Erasmus: 'I had rather see with my own eyes than with those of
others, and in the next place, much as they have said [that is, the
old interpreters] they have left much to be said by posterity.'[10] In
this preface Erasmus is using Valla as a weapon against the forces
of mere traditionalism; here he shows the need for going to the
sources, and correcting the Vulgate by the Greek original, even to
providing a new translation more correct and more appropriate to
the present time. To us this seems the reasonable and desirable
activity of sound scholarship, but in 1505 these proposals were
revolutionary. The Greek original was regarded as the biased
authority of schismatical, if not heterodox, Greeks: to use their
Greek original was to favour their dangerous opinions. Again it
was assumed that the making of the Vulgate Latin version had
been guided by the inspiration of the Holy Spirit; it had been
sanctified by eleven hundred years of use in the Latin Church; and
it was most intimately related to the most sacred traditions of
worship, piety and doctrine. Many thought that to turn aside to
the Greek was not only unnecessary, it would begin the dissolu-
tion of Catholic authority. The full weight of this traditionalist

attack would fall on Erasmus from 1516 after his edition of the New Testament appeared. In that year, however, Froben, the same printer, published the works of Jerome for which Erasmus had been the chief among the editors. Erasmus could now face the challenge, which he knew was coming, with the formidable support of Jerome.

Erasmus showed both courage and integrity in carrying through to fulfilment, in these labours, his years of devotion to Jerome and to the principles of Valla, and in thus challenging scholasticism, obscurantism and the superstitions of popular piety. He stubbornly maintained his position on the New Testament, and on his annotations to it, until his death a year after the fifth edition of the work amid serious hostility and amid increasing difficulties. If some degree of mild persecution mania suggests itself, it is not altogether surprising in view of these problems—for instance, he seems to have had a rule that when in doubt of the source of an attack he should blame Cardinal Aleandro.[11] Alongside of his scholar's courage, however, there was a certain deviousness, or, less pejoratively, a certain skill in manoeuvre in seeking to disarm his enemies and to explain away acerbities by sheltering behind great or respected names, for example, the Bishop of Cambrai, Archbishop Warham, and Pope Leo X; John Colet who would impress the English; and Sir Thomas More who had both an English and a European reputation. Like the English Fabians of the 1890s he wrote manifestos announcing a new way of life, and like them he was unwilling by temperament, and because of his chosen method, to see this way introduced by violent means. But he certainly produced the manifestos though he later showed the uncommitted intellectual's shock when men used them in a revolutionary way as, for example, von Hutten did in Germany. Two of his most significant writings of this challenging kind were the introduction to the New Testament, the *Paraclesis*, and his life of Jerome used as an introduction to Froben's edition of the collected works of Jerome. This life of Jerome shows Erasmus as the cunctative revolutionary challenging the dying middle ages in religion, learning, piety and social order, in the name of the saint whom he admired more than any other of the Fathers and Doctors of the Church. He may have thought of writing it to provide a protective shield for his own work, but his pen moulded it into a weapon of attack.

The *Life of Jerome* is a powerful attempt to establish the facts while at the same time ignoring the traditional envelope of hagiography. It is hardly a product of his earlier studies in Jerome, for it is the result of mature work on and deep knowledge of the writings of Jerome. On his second visit to England in 1509 he had lectured on the letters of Jerome, and three years later Badius at Paris wrote to Erasmus asking if he could publish Erasmus' edition of these letters. But by the end of 1513 he was attracted to the presses of Amorbach and Froben at Basel who planned to publish the whole of Jerome's works. Froben persuaded Erasmus to guide the editorial team and to be himself responsible for the letters. In the event Erasmus achieved more than this since he added notes to the text and provided the *Life* as an introduction. In the *Life of Jerome* Erasmus introduced a different method in writing the life of a saint, and the characteristic accretions of legend in hagiography were firmly set aside. The new departure here was that Erasmus used nothing save the earliest and best records: 'I think there is nothing fairer than to describe saints of the kind of which they themselves were, as men in whose lives even the discovery of anything wrong can be turned into an example of goodness. . . . But who could endure those who with ravings worse than those of old women, children, illiterates, and fools do not exalt the saints but rather drag them down?'[12] Erasmus then states that he will use only the most trustworthy sources written by Jerome's contemporaries Prosper, Severus, Orosius, Rufinus and that even more diligence would be given to tracing out the life of Jerome from his own writings. In scorn, for example, of the pious stories in the Golden Legend, he added that those who wished to find miracles in Jerome's life would do better to read his works which are themselves as it were miraculous. It is unfortunate, though perhaps inevitable in view of the state of exact learning at the time, that Erasmus began the *Life* with an error of his own in stating that Jerome was born under the Emperor Constantine instead of Constantius, and produced some other minor misunderstandings on times, persons and places.

Erasmus found an opportunity in the *Life* to point more than one contemporary moral, thus underlining its quality of being a manifesto. This soon appears when he wrote that it was to Jerome's youthful training in 'good letters' that we owe an incomparable Doctor of the Church 'non loquacium sophistarum scholis'.[13] In the vocabulary of Erasmus sophist was an alternative word for barbarian to describe a scholastic theologian. Erasmus points another moral when he contrasts contemporary monasticism with that of Jerome's time: '. . . quod ne quis in hoc erret, id temporis longe diversum erat ac hoc quod hodie videmus caerimoniis obstrictum . . .'[14] Again Jerome was, of course, not a cardinal though iconography showed him in a cardinal's hat and the tradition of his being a cardinal-priest is echoed in the Golden Legend, but Erasmus is quick both to point out the error and to make the comment that the splendour and dignity of cardinals in the sixteenth century were unknown in Jerome's time. In describing Jerome as receiving by night the Jew Bar Hanina to teach Jerome Hebrew, like another Nicodemus coming secretly to avoid the hatred of the Jews, Erasmus would touch many a contemporary scholar, for this expensive procedure was still employed by Christians seeking to learn Hebrew—he himself had possibly used it. It was this continuous suggestion of contemporaneity with the past which gave the living quality to the *Life*. For fifteenth-century writers the men of the fourth century had been clothed in forms appropriate to medieval culture: Erasmus toiled to place Jerome exactly in his true period, using the scholarship available to him with the greatest skill, and in doing so he made Jerome more alive and more contemporary because he made him appropriate to an age of humanism and not of medievalism. That Erasmus wrote in favour of Biblical humanism and the priority of trilingual learning can be seen in his taking for granted what was in fact not true, that Augustine must have consistently disliked Jerome; for Erasmus saw Augustine, while respecting him for his greatness, as the father of that dogmatic theology which he himself distrusted. Erasmus is equally committed, as though it were in his own quarrel, when he attacked Rufinus, whom he unjustly saw as being wholly wrong in his opposition to Jerome: but no doubt he saw in Rufinus Jerome's Aleandro. The *Life of Jerome* gradually moved to a climax by becoming more and more a contemporary document. Erasmus indignantly attacked the scholastics for denying that Jerome was a theologian and demoting him to being a mere grammarian, 'because he does not crackle with majors and minors' like the followers of Scotus.[15] He paused to exclaim:

Who could have guessed that this kind of theology would develop among Christians? . . . Who would guess that there would be those who would refashion the whole of theology from head to heel, as they say, and make out of what had been a heavenly subject something Sophistic, Thomistic, or Scotist, or Occamist? ... What a calamity for Christendom, which had managed for more than a thousand years without theologians![16]

The *Life* concludes with a vigorous defence of good letters grounded on trilingual learning and on scriptural piety against scholastic divinity, and against half-pagan Ciceronianism. Here Erasmus aims his blows at contemporary Italian humanists (generally somewhat suspect to the more sober Biblical humanism of northern Europe) whose names crackle through these sentences like abusive expletives—one example is his tart rebuke of Filippo Beroaldo for criticizing Jerome's taste in using the words 'pexa tunica'. For good measure he added the lyrical statement that Bethlehem was twice happy since there Christ was born for the world and Jerome was born for heaven. 'There was no kind of teaching which here cannot be aided, no foundation of life which cannot be embellished by his precepts', and Erasmus dourly concluded, 'Jerome hated and abhorred heretics, those alone he had for his bitterest enemies',[17] to show that he aligned himself with ancient orthodoxy and implied a warning that criticism of Biblical humanism might in turn be challenged as heresy.

This *Life* and the edition of Jerome's Works, while they were a powerful demonstration of the status and significance of Biblical humanism, could not be in themselves a justification of Erasmus as a trilingual scholar. We have to go elsewhere to examine his competence in Greek and Hebrew. It would not have been obvious to those who knew him that in 1499 he would turn from concentrating on classical studies to the Biblical languages. We must allow for the hidden and slow gestation of genius, and not look for a lightning flash of decision by which to determine precisely where, when and why Erasmus made this change of direction. It should not be forgotten, moreover, that Erasmus never lost touch with the piety of his youthful environment, and was always a moralist. But it was probably in 1499, on his first visit to England, that he made up his mind to take up these new studies. There is no proof of it, but it was most probably his friendship with the single-minded and devout John Colet that helped him towards this change. Colet himself knew Greek imperfectly and no Hebrew, yet he lectured on the Bible urging that from this starting point alone could new insights into the Christian faith begin. Colet's concentration on Biblically grounded Christian values, his contempt for popular superstitions, and his scorn for scholastic theologians (not excluding Aquinas whom Erasmus had thought it expedient to praise) impressed the less committed Erasmus. He left England for Paris determined to master Greek, for he was now fully convinced that through this language the mind would be enlarged, that men could break free from the iron bands of scholastic latinity with more assurance by its means. The task before him, and so many other younger aspirants to trilingual learning at that time, was formidable. Teachers were few, expensive and educationally incompetent: the university faculties ignored and distrusted these studies; and grammars and dictionaries barely existed. Aldus Manutius had published the Greek grammar of the Byzantine refugee Lascaris in 1495 but there was little else of use. Men would have to wait until 1520 for the thorough though complex *Commentarii Linguae Graecae* of Guillaume Budé at Paris, and a useful dictionary did not appear until the *Lexicon Graeco-Latinum* published at Paris in 1530. Only the intensely dedicated could track their way through the forest of difficulties in studying Greek outside Italy in 1500. Lack of resources and the pressure of patronage allowed Erasmus to go no further than Paris.

In April 1500 he wrote to Batt that he was applying his whole mind to learning Greek, spending what little money he had first on Greek books, with clothing coming a late second.[18] To another friend from whom he had borrowed a copy of Homer he wrote that year saying he burned with love for the author but was unable to understand him effectively.[19] There must be a touch of modesty here, for an admiring pupil records that Erasmus produced some excellent Latin translations from the Odyssey at that time. In any case Erasmus had very probably acquired the elements of Greek in his youth; his problem in 1499 had been that he knew he had no real grip on the language. At Paris he found a teacher in George Hermonymus of Sparta, as we learn from his autobiographical letter to Botzheim over twenty years later, where he adds that when he began there were hardly any books in Greek available, and even fewer teachers of it. Of this master he could say no more than that he stammered the language and was twice a Greek in being always greedy and charging a high salary: this no doubt

means that while Hermonymus spoke Greek he had no professional grasp of teaching method, and of grammatical exposition.[20]
But in 1501 Erasmus was deep in Lascaris' Greek grammar, and
also worked through that of the Italian master in Greek of Leo X,
the Franciscan Bolzani. With the excitement of discovery he
showed a friend that year how in Psalm 50 a knowledge of Greek
could transform meaningfully a passage of Scripture otherwise
misleading and obscure in Latin. (His weakness in Hebrew shows
why he used the Septuagint Greek for the Old Testament):

> Who could understand the sentence in the Psalm, 'Et peccatum
> meum contra me est semper', unless he has read the Greek? This
> runs as follows, καὶ ἡ ἁμαρτία μου ἐνώπιόν μου ἐστὶ διαπαντός. At
> this point some theologian will spin a long story of how the flesh
> is perpetually in conflict with the spirit, having been misled by the
> double meaning of the preposition, that is, *contra*, when the word
> ἐνώπιον refers not to 'conflict' but to 'position', as if you were to
> say 'opposite', that is, 'in sight': so that the prophet's meaning was
> that his fault was so hateful to him that the memory of it never left
> him, but floated always before his mind as if it were present.[21]

The following year his tense concentration is shown in the words
'in Graecis litteris sum totus'.[22] By 1506 he had published Valla's
annotations on the Greek New Testament, and he was publishing
his own Latin version of certain plays by Euripides.

That Erasmus widened and deepened his Greek learning in his
visits to Italy and to England in the sixteen years up to 1516
should not overshadow his achievement in the period 1499–1505
which is a record of intense devotion to his conception of his life's
work. Those sixteen years of labour show that he had learned to
use Greek with something of that familiarity with which he had
previously learned to use Latin as a living language. This sense of
the past as if it were restored to life in the present enabled Erasmus
to give contemporaneity to the Greek writings of what he believed
to be the golden age of the Church.

He held also to the Greek pagan writers of the Empire, Lucian
—whom he warmly recommended to the students of the trilingual
college of Busleiden at Louvain—and Plutarch, preferring them to
Aristotle and to a less degree to Plato. Just as he showed little
interest in Christian mysticism so he was unattracted by the Italian
enthusiasm for reading Plato through the haze of neo-Platonism, a
fashion which captured Jacques Lefèvre and even affected Colet's
pragmatic mind. Erasmus delighted in Lucian's irony, and his

genius for social criticism in dramatic dialogue; and Plutarch attracted his interest through his handling of men's histories within the frame of moral criticism. The great philosophical tradition of Greece was for him too speculative and too dialectical. These attitudes to Greek learning can be seen too in his lack of the profound philological concern of Guillaume Budé, and of the paedagogic zeal of the young Melanchthon.

He also attempted to learn Hebrew in pursuit of his ideal of being like Jerome a trilingual scholar. Possibly he had tried it earlier, but by 1503 he sadly concedes that he had undertaken too much at his age. 'I began also to look into Hebrew, but I was put off by the strangeness of the language, and also because neither my age nor my ability can handle several things at once, I gave up.'[23] The difficulty here was even more formidable than with Greek, as no satisfactory grammars or dictionaries yet existed in forms suitable for non-Jewish beginners. A small volume had been produced by Pellican at Strasburg in 1503, and while the German Biblical humanist Reuchlin could claim to be the first who opened the way for non-Jews to learn Hebrew in his *De Rudimentis Linguae Hebraicae* in 1506, it was no wonder of scholarship, for it contained some errors and obscurities. A good dictionary was also lacking for some years to come. When he was working on the text of Jerome's Works in 1515 for Froben, Erasmus found a number of Hebrew words and phrases in the Biblical commentaries of Jerome, and he confessed 'these letters I had barely more than tasted and scarcely touched upon'.[24] In the Preface to Jerome's Works he stated that he had had to find help from the three sons of Amorbach: 'Quorum equidem auxilio libenter sum usus, quod Hebraeorum literas degustassem verius quam dedicissem.'[25] Again he had to rely on Froben's proof-reader, Oecolampadius, who was later to become the Protestant reformer at Basel, for similar help where necessary with those Hebrew words he desired to consider in his notes to the Greek-Latin New Testament he published at Basel in 1516. In 1517 Erasmus has a vague reference to his taking some Hebrew lessons at Louvain, probably from Cellarius, but this effort soon faded, and we hear no more of his Hebrew studies.[26]

In Hebrew studies, in contrast with the competence he achieved in Greek, he got no further than the basic paradigms: almost certainly he could not have accurately provided with the vowel-points a consonantal text, nor could he have followed the intricacies of the Hebrew verbs. In his exegesis of passages from the Old Testament, where one would have expected him to refer to the Hebrew text, he almost wholly ignores it, and relies on the Septuagint Greek. In his annotations of the New Testament and in helping to edit Jerome's exegetical works, where Hebrew words were cited, he had assistance as shown above from scholars working for Froben's press.

Inside so many of the humanists of his own and of the succeeding generation a pedant was struggling, sometimes successfully, to get out. Erasmus, however, achieved 'humanitas' as a style of living as well as of writing: for him pursuing scholarship into pedantry was a deviation from a reasonable norm. This is part of his attraction as a writer but it had the regrettable consequence that he lacked the perfectionism of the pure scholar; while he had insight and originality, he was careless about precision in a reading, the collation of texts and painstaking care in interpreting them. The scholar's perfectionism in detail was for him a rare achievement—Erasmus was not a Housman. With his literary flair rather than scholarly precision in handling Greek texts, and with the weakness in Hebrew, which he himself acknowledged, he was not the most suitable editor of a Biblical text. The editors of the text of the New Testament in the Complutensian Polyglot Bible, printed though not published in 1514, produced more careful and significant work, and Simon de Colines, either through his own skills or more probably through the work of a scholar otherwise unknown to us, printed what was a great deal better version of the text of the Greek New Testament at Paris in 1535 than Erasmus had achieved in five editions by that year. But where Erasmus gained all Europe's attention was in the boldness and vigour of his Latin translation from the Greek and his annotations, especially since these were written by the author of the *Enchiridion* and the *Moriae Encomium*. A generation of converts to the 'New Learning' grew up with Erasmus' editions of the New Testament. But some of this generation came to wonder whether all the skill of Erasmus in writing, his freedom from anachronisms and from the scholastic manifold meanings of even the literal sense of Scripture, had sufficiently covered his lack of theological depth and energy in his interpretations, and his casual methods of emending the Greek text—scholars of his own generation publicly expressed their doubts, including the powerful names of Luther and Stunica. Moreover, the toils of Browning's Grammarian were not for Erasmus: he had mocked the consequences of such labours in his *Moriae Encomium*. His gifts lay in creating new insights, and in the art of literary allusion (in which he was almost as wide-ranging as the Deipnosophists of Athenaeus), and not in the technical scholarship necessary for the editing of texts.

Frequently the excuse is made for him that this skill was unknown in his time, but someone used it in preparing the text of de Colines' Greek New Testament; and the Christian Hebraists of Alcalá de Henares prepared after some years of effort the Hebrew text of the Old Testament in the Complutensian Polyglot Bible, which is still of interest to scholars. Erasmus might have created a thirst for better scholarship through the potent attraction of his name and of his edition of the New Testament, so that younger men could have done better what he had done imperfectly, if it had not been for the fact that both Catholics and Protestants, locked in an exhausting and inconclusive struggle to demonstrate each other's errors, ended by mid-century in that theological authoritarianism which Erasmus feared would develop from Luther's protest. In this situation there could be little scholarly advance; what was achieved was greater precision but with narrowed insights. The excessive caution shown by Beza in his edition of the text of the Greek New Testament (when he had the Western text before him to show him new possibilities) demonstrates this in the second half of the century.

It is probable that Erasmus first thought of preparing annotations to the Greek New Testament when he prepared those of Lorenzo Valla for the press in 1505, and it is even more probable that in the same period he began to consider preparing his own Latin version of the Greek New Testament, but it was not until 1512–13, while he was in England, that he decided to prepare an edition of the Greek text.[27] It is very difficult to disentangle his allusions to the preparation of his annotations but they seem to have been put together in a desultory manner (though he was busy with them in August 1514 as a letter to Reuchlin shows)[28] probably to accompany his proposed new Latin version, though they were made upon the Vulgate text, and in the event a considerable number of them were prepared while the first edition of the New Testament was in the press at Basel in 1515: 'Then they

induced me to add much more copious annotations.'[29] But there
is clear evidence concerning his preparation of a new Latin version, for a magnificent copy of it exists containing the gospels and
epistles made by the scribe Peter Meghen, on Colet's orders,
during 1506–9.

Another manuscript of this version exists which is interlined
with the Vulgate, and is less magnificent though probably dating
from the same period.[30] Undoubtedly Colet persuaded Erasmus
to begin translating the Greek New Testament in 1505 and most
probably the task was completed by 1506: these statements do not
require the view that Erasmus intended to publish this version at
that period; it was not until 1514 that he began to consider
issuing this version with his edition of the Greek New Testament
and accompanying annotations. His preparation of the Greek
text is less easy to determine, but there are occasional references
to his working on it and it is probable that he had begun collating
Greek manuscripts by 1512–13 if not earlier, for he wrote from
London in September 1512 to Peter Gilles, 'absolvam castiga-
tiones Novi Testamenti ...' Again in July 1514 he wrote to
Servatius Rogerius: 'Ex Graecorum et antiquorum codicum
collatione castigavi totum Novum Testamentum ... commentarios in Epistolas Pauli incepi, quos absolvam ubi haec edidero.'[31]

From July 1514 to March 1515 Erasmus was at Basel but no
evidence is available that he thought of publishing there his Latin
New Testament with annotations during this period. Possibly he
had been thinking of an Italian publisher, perhaps Aldus Manutius
who had been the first printer of his *Adagia* and to whom he had
written in October 1507 wondering why he did not publish the
New Testament. But a sense of urgency developed when Froben,
it is conjectured, heard of the completion of the printing of the
Greek New Testament at Alcalá de Henares in 1514 (left unbound
in sheets awaiting the publication of the whole work) and that the
editors were pressing on with the Old Testament of the Polyglot
Bible. Beatus Rhenanus wrote to Erasmus twice in April 1515 to
say that Froben would like to publish the edition of the New
Testament which Erasmus was known to be preparing, on the
first occasion adding that Froben would offer a price equal to that
of any other printer. It is not explicit that both the Greek text and
the new Latin version of Erasmus were intended in these brief
sentences, but since Erasmus wrote to Wimpfeling in September

1514: 'Superest Novum Testamentum a me versum et e regione Graecum . . .';[32] and again to Cardinal Grimani in May 1515[33] that he had in mind to publish commentaries on the Pauline epistles following in the steps of Valla and Lefèvre d'Etaples, he was now probably considering the preparation of a Greek text to accompany the Latin version and the commentary. What emerges from these tantalizing and inexplicit surviving references to his preparing to publish the New Testament, is that Erasmus for some time intended to prepare no more than his new Latin version with annotations in the method of Valla, and that the decision to publish the Greek text to accompany these was taken much later and probably at Froben's suggestion. In the event he had less than a year, at a time when he was also pressed with other work, to prepare the Greek text for publication.

Erasmus claimed on the title page of the work, again in a declaration at the end, and more fully and confidently still in the dedicatory letter to Leo X, that he had used many old and correct manuscripts of the Greek text as well as citations of the New Testament text made by the Greek Fathers. This is disingenuous. He could claim from the generously disposed that he meant that he had consulted some old manuscripts when he had been preparing his notes, but the implications of the language he used in the passages mentioned was that he had edited the printed Greek text by the careful collation of a number of ancient manuscripts—and this was not true, or at best it was no more than a half-truth. In the short time he allowed himself for the preparation of the whole work for the printers, together with his seeing through the press his Jerome and other writings, he had little opportunity to collate and refine. He did no more than to deliver in the first place to the printers two manuscripts, one of the gospels, and one of the epistles, which he found to his hand at Basel, and which are still preserved in that city. The general consensus of scholars has considered these to be of late origin possibly as late as the fifteenth century. He himself recognized that they were defective in textual value, and complained to Budé that he had had to make corrections in them before sending them to Froben's compositors after a hasty comparison with a few other manuscripts at Basel. Since the book of *Revelation* was lacking in the second manuscript he gave to the printers, he used another manuscript lent to him by Reuchlin, which also still survives. Because the Biblical text was connected with a commentary in Greek in this manuscript, Erasmus had to make a copy himself of the actual text of *Revelation* contained in the manuscript, but he did not do this with the necessary care since he failed to correct some false readings. Further the manuscript lacked the last five verses of *Revelation* and he translated these verses into his own Greek from the Vulgate text (he also added at *Acts* 8[37] and *Acts* 9[5-6] Greek not to be found in the manuscripts). He admitted this in the Annotations but, again disingenuously, or possibly ignorantly, suggested that he is translating some words which do not appear in the Greek. Also in the Annotations he cited readings from manuscripts he had consulted in different cities in the years in which he had been preparing his Latin version. Since a few of these readings have not been found in any manuscripts since, it may be possible that he made some independent readings of his own, or else he was relying on defective memory.

Not only was the text hastily prepared but also the printers were careless in their work. That twelve pages, a ternion, were printed daily shows the haste of the compositors, and the pressure on the proof-readers, Nicholas Gerbel and Oecolampadius, whom Erasmus blamed in the following year somewhat ungenerously since both were competent in Greek and zealous for the good of the work.[34] Printing had begun in October 1515 and the whole work was completed and published in March 1516. But this important and influential edition was half-hidden under a cloud of typographical and other errors: 501 itacisms have been counted which were taken over from the manuscripts into the printed text. The perfectionism of later textual criticism looked on this Greek text—which formed part of the foundation of the 'textus receptus' for four centuries—with dubiety. And Scrivener wrote of its typographical errors, 'the first edition is the most faulty book I know'.[35] This is applying too harshly later standards of typographical and scholarly precision to the early sixteenth century, but Erasmus was also challenged for his casualness in his own time. Erasmus was not exaggerating when he admitted that this work, which was to have so great an influence on his time, nevertheless, 'praecipitatum est verius quam aeditum'; but he could also write to a friend 'Aeditum est pro temporis angustia satis accurate',[36] which does not suggest that he was much perturbed by its precipitate appearance.

The new Latin translation which Erasmus provided to accompany the Greek text showed that greater care had been given to this text, which he had been working on at different periods for longer than he worked at the editing of the Greek text. It should not be overlooked that the excitement caused by this edition of the New Testament was also occasioned by the Latin version made by Erasmus, and the accompanying annotations. Not only was the publication of the Greek text a new departure, but also it was new boldly to set aside the Vulgate, the authoritative version, hallowed by tradition for Christian thought, worship, and piety, in favour of this product of contemporary latinity. The impact of this version can be seen in the tragedy of Thomas Bilney, Fellow of Trinity Hall, Cambridge, burned for heresy at Norwich in 1531, who was set on the road leading him to death by fire as a Protestant martyr through his admiration for this Latin version of Erasmus which led him into deeper theological waters than he had known of before. (He could have benefited little from the Greek text because of the weakness of Greek studies in England at that time.) Bilney wrote to Cuthbert Tunstall, bishop of London, in 1527 giving an account of the change thus made in him years before: '. . . At last I heard speak of Jesus, even then when the New Testament was set forth by Erasmus; which when I understood to be eloquently done by him, being allured rather by the Latin than by the word of God (for at that time I knew not what it meant), I bought it even by the providence of God. . . .'[37] In this he was one of a large company of young men whose lives were set on different courses (not only towards Protestantism, but also towards Catholic reformist ideals) by this Greek-Latin New Testament of Erasmus: a whole generation of young scholars was roused by it. That Bilney was 'allured by the Latin' would have pleased Erasmus—though Bilney's Protestantism would not—for he claimed that he had prepared his Latin version not for common use but as a help to those who were professionally students of theology: 'non ita scribuntur multitudine sed eruditis et praecipiis Theologiae candidatis'. This was no doubt an attempt to anticipate the attack on his boldness in setting aside the Vulgate in favour of his own version, just as he sought to play down potential hostility to his annotations by stating that they were not theological commentaries.

His new Latin version, however, not only expressed his concern for contemporary standards of latinity, but also his genuine principles in setting aside the Vulgate. Erasmus had written years before to Archbishop Warham in a letter published as a preface to his translation of two plays by Euripides: 'The mere task of putting real Greek into real Latin is such that it requires an extraordinary artist, and not only a man with a rich store of scholarship in both languages at his fingertips, but one exceedingly alert and observant'.[38] He wished to make the Greek as clear as possible, it was not enough to give a bare literal version for this can obscure the meaning, and he defended his recent Latin Paraphrases of the New Testament as clarifying the difficulties of New Testament idiom for the inexpert reader. In a letter of August 1518 to Antony Pucci, at the time papal nuncio in Switzerland, he wrote:

> We placed our translation by the side of the Greek text, so that the reader might readily compare the two, the translation being so made, that it was our first study to preserve, as far as was permissible, the integrity of the Latin tongue without injury to the simplicity of the apostolic language. Our next care was to provide that any sentences which had before given trouble to the reader, either by ambiguity or obscurity of language, or by faulty or unsuitable expressions, should be explained and made clear with as little deviation as possible from the words of the original, and none from the sense.[39]

In the annotations he showed the problems created by the Vulgate rendering, and gave reasons for his own translation where it differed from the Vulgate: as he noted in his *Apologia* (one of the four preliminary portions, Dedication to Leo X, *Paraclesis*, *Ratio seu Methodus*, and *Apologia*, set before these editions) his purpose was not to replace the official wording—essential to the authoritative transactions of the Church—but to send his own version forth as a help to understanding better the Vulgate. But in spite of his ingenuous hope he was, in the eyes of his critics, undermining by his methods in translation and annotation the authority of the Vulgate.

His version, he insisted, for he did not wish it to be misconceived as consciously literary, was to be seen rather as clear and plain, 'non tam elegantius, quam dilucidus ac fidelius'.[40] A version nearer to showing the Bible 'designed to be read as literature', in twentieth-century phrase, was not to come until that of Sebastian Castellio forty years later. Nevertheless, for Bilney it was the allurement of the Latin which provided the first attraction; and no one who glances through three consecutive pages of the Latin version and the accompanying notes could miss the Erasmian *suavitas* and the conscious pleasure in classical allusions—in a word style. Perhaps Erasmus did not realize how revolutionary could be the effect of his style and method: his version of the New Testament made it seem like a new discovery, new threads of unsuspected meanings could be unwound with increasing excitement. For the most famous of German jurists, the humanist scholar Zazius, this version of Erasmus gave clearer sense and better Latin than the Vulgate. He seemed to have created a new Biblical language, for in his version the inhibiting traces of Hebrew and Greek idiom almost disappeared; and his short preparatory treatises were read as manifestos challenging the language, methods, and even the principles of a traditionalism grounded on an increasingly barren scholasticism. John Watson, Fellow of Peterhouse and soon to be Vice-Chancellor of Cambridge University, represents one of a great number of enthusiastic greetings fired by this freshness of insight obtained on the publication of the work: 'By your correction of the New Testament accompanied by your annotations you have thrown a marvellous light on Christ, and deserved well of all his zealous followers.'[41]

These annotations were both part of the fascination of the work, and also the ground for some of the bitterest attacks upon it. Here Erasmus demonstrated what was no more than implicit in his new Latin version, that there were errors and obscurities in the Vulgate. But also something of the style and manner of the notes to his *Adagia*, so attractive to his contemporaries, with their illuminating digressions and complete mastery of classical learning, could be found in the annotations. For those who attacked him there was more of literature than theological exegesis in them. However, in the preface to his readers Erasmus had provided a defence in advance by describing them as 'annotatiunculas ... non commentarios'. The favour long given to the New Testament commentary of Thomas Aquinas would be shaken, in the eyes of many rudely challenged, by a mere grammarian when Erasmus wrote 'Thomas hoc loco se torquet', and the phrases 'Thomas frustra philosophans in loco depravato, Thomas lapsus, Thomas lapsus miserandus, Thomae annotatio ridicula' appear in marginal references and index; whereas only once 'Thomas laudatus' appears. On that most controverted topic of the time, the Pauline doctrine of Predestination, about which he wrestled with Luther in his *De Libero Arbitrio*, Erasmus can say little more in a note on *Romans* VIII than, 'Nor am I ignorant that there are certain persons, who on this passage seek a field for exercising their ingenuity and philosophize on the foreknowledge and predestination of God', and added with irony 'of their diligence I do not disapprove'. Those who took for granted the plain authority of the word of God were alarmed at his note on *Romans* IX. 5, where he showed that the obscurity of the Greek offers no clear rejection of Arianism since the words 'benedictus in secula' may refer not to Christ, as was usually understood, but to God the Father. Even more serious was his omission of *I John* V.7 in the first two editions of his Greek version, for the soundest of critical reasons that it was not in the early manuscripts: the note on the text in the later editions was not considered helpful any more than his long note on *John* I. 1, justifying his use of 'sermo' for 'verbum', in the edition of 1519. Equally serious in the eyes of many were his digressive comments, sometimes ironical, more often Erasmus at his most serious, on what he regarded as scandals in the lives of the Christians of his own time: on the vestments and ceremonies of the Church, on marriage, divorce and the possible modification of clerical celibacy, on penance and the use of relics, and on various aspects of monasticism and the making of vows. There were those outside of the sodalities of 'good letters', which accepted Erasmus gladly, who could be seriously offended at his scornful listing of 'Mary's milk exhibited in our churches for money; Francis's hood shown at one altar and the Virgin Mary's shift at another; in one Church Anna's comb, in another Joseph's boot,' and so on.[42] Further, the comment, removed from later editions, on Peter lodging with Simon the tanner (*Acts* IX. 43): 'the chief of the Apostles to lodge with so humble a host; in our time three royal palaces barely suffice to receive Peter's vicar', would challenge customary deference as did other similar ironies on the Papacy.

More serious occasions for alarm were given when Erasmus was found to have proposed corrections to the Vulgate text; and, worse, suggested that certain passages in the gospels were of doubtful authenticity; and equally dangerously questioned whether texts traditionally used in support of long-held dogmas could be read in this way. He corrected the latinity of the Vulgate when he rejected its version of *John* XVI. 13 'docebit vos omnem veritatem' to read 'ducet ($\delta\delta\eta\gamma\dot{\eta}\sigma\epsilon\iota$) vos in omnem veritatem'. He drew attention to the probability that the last twelve verses of the gospel of Mark were inauthentic, and also argued the same on the passage *John* VII. 53–VIII. 11, the story of the woman taken in adultery, since it was absent from the early patristic references to John's gospel, and from the best manuscripts: both his critical acumen and his courage are equally praiseworthy in maintaining in later editions that these passages might well be interpolations. He undermined traditional dogmatic proof-texts when he translated μετανοεῖτε, in the annotations as 'resipiscite' or 'ad mentem redite' thereby drawing attention to the ambiguity in the Vulgate rendering 'penitentiam agite', since the noun means both 'repentance' and 'penance'—an ambiguity essential to the then current Catholic interpretation of the Sacrament of Penance. At several other places Erasmus indicated that the Vulgate text did not provide those proofs of dogmas for which it was frequently adduced. At *Romans* V. 12, he gave a lengthy note of six and a half pages challenging the traditional doctrine of original sin and its derivation from the sin of Adam. At *Romans* IX. 5, *Philippians* II. 6, *Colossians* XI. 9, he undermined the value of their use against Arianism; and at *I Timothy* III. 16, he argued θεός had been added later to make the text explicit against the Arians. He curtly challenged the current view of merit when he wrote under *Titus* II. 11, 'non merito nostro salvati simus' in discussing briefly the saving grace of God.

Under *Matthew* II, Erasmus stated that the writers of the gospels might have erred in not examining the books they quoted or paraphrased, and trusted too much to memory. After this it would appear less startling to learn that he thought Mark was merely a compendium of Matthew, that Luke was not an eye-witness, that the epistle of James lacked apostolic majesty and probably apostolic authority, that *Hebrews* was not by Paul (could it have been written by Clement of Rome he asked?), and, why should it be in the canon?, and lastly, did the heretic Cerinthus write *Revelation*, for John surely could not have done so? Amid these heady themes it was a relief to his opponents that his own work as an annotator was not impeccable and they gladly pointed out his occasional geographical errors (for example, his assumption on *Acts* XVI. 11, that the port of Neapolis was a town in Caria, in Asia instead of Macedonia), and his weakness in Hebrew was noted, for example, when he introduced a curious lady called Tabitha in misreading

the Aramaic 'Talitha cumi' at *Mark* V. 41—almost as curious as
his invention of a non-existent church Father unfortunately named
Vulgarius by Erasmus, who had apparently misread βουλγαρίας as
βουλγαρίου and read θεοφυλάκτου as a descriptive adjective in the
title in a manuscript copy of a commentary on Matthew by the
Byzantine Theophylact of Bulgaria. Among these sharp critics of
his work on the New Testament were first in the field two
Englishmen; a Franciscan, Henry Standish, who was promoted
bishop of St Asaph (a fact which gave Erasmus the opportunity of
describing him as 'episcopus de St Asino'), and Edward Lee,
later Archbishop of York. Dr Standish, preaching at Paul's Cross,
usually a sounding board for official views in Church and State,
informed the mildly surprised Lord Mayor and Corporation that
the total extinction of Christianity was at hand, and wept like
Tweedledee's Walrus, to relate that Erasmus could alter *John* I. 1,
to 'in principio erat sermo'.[43] Dr Lee was much more formidable.
He produced a book of criticisms in spite of threats from Erasmus,
who had learned of the forthcoming work beforehand, that he
would be supported by his German friends 'who still retained
their native ferocity'.[44] Lee rightly complained of the casual haste
with which Erasmus had edited the text, introduced unusual views
in his annotations, and occasionally translated what was absent
from the Greek in his own Latin version—and expressed outrage
not least at Erasmus providing some Greek of his own to conclude *Revelation*.[45] Even more formidable was the Spaniard, Diego
Lopez de Zuñiga (Stunica), an able editor of the Greek New
Testament printed for the magnificent Polyglot Bible at Alcalá de
Henares (Complutum) in 1514, though unpublished until eight
years later. Stunica must have taken it hard that what he rightly
knew was a better text, better prepared and edited by himself and
his colleagues, already printed in sheets in 1514, failed to achieve
priority in publication through the delay of Leo X in licensing
their Bible, and instead saw the renown and popularity which
Erasmus had achieved by his hastily issued edition. Stunica, from
the high chair of his own undoubted trilingual learning, attacked
Erasmus at the lowest level for being a typical Dutchman soaked
in beer and butter, who had won some renown in literature
particularly, he wrote ominously, for his studies in proverbs and
the works of Lucian; and at the higher level drew attention to the
deficiencies of Erasmus' editing of the Greek text.[46] It was some

tribute to Stunica's critical acumen (in spite of his unwarrantable defence of a number of places in the Vulgate against what he thought of as the Arianizing of Erasmus) that Erasmus silently corrected a number of errors pointed out by Stunica in later editions of his New Testament.

Erasmus was not done with his labours on the New Testament after 1516 when, in that year, he wrote to Pirckheimer, 'in the labour house at Basel' he had done the work of six years in eight months. From June 1517 he began to reflect upon the second edition in the event not wholly overseen by himself, and by the end of the year he wrote to another friend: 'Here I am once more in this hateful mill'.[47] This edition was published in 1519 and was, however, really a corrected reprint of the former edition for which only one new Greek manuscript was used, with some revised notes; moreover new faults are found among the corrected old ones. Now appeared, without any modifications to accommodate with the Vulgate in the gospels, as he did in the first edition, the original wholly Erasmian Latin version which has been considered above; and there appeared also the more traditional title *Novum Testamentum* instead of the unusual *Novum Instrumentum* of his first edition. The famous short treatise 'Ratio seu Compendium verae Theologiae' was now set before the second edition and a reply to his detractors 'Capita argumentorum contra morosos quosdam ac indoctos'. Another edition appeared in 1522 which included the *Comma Joanneum* (I John V. 7) after Stunica's fierce attack, on the weak admission that he had found it in one Greek manuscript (minuscule 61) at last—now long since known to be a late interpolation there—with some corrections too from the Complutensian Polyglot and the addition of the Vulgate version alongside his own. The fourth edition came in 1527 and the fifth and last edition in Erasmus' lifetime came in the year before his death, 1535, with a few minor alterations to the fourth.

Erasmus tried to forestall the developing attack on him, which he learned of from various friends in England and elsewhere, by writing in the *Contra Morosos ac Indoctos* published in the 1519 edition, that he had never wished to depart by a finger or nail's breadth from the judgment of the Catholic Church. But an opponent of long-standing, the Carmelite Nicholas Egmond, who according to Erasmus had turned Cardinal Aleandro against him, an impassioned antagonist of trilingual learning, asserted that

Erasmus' New Testament foreshadowed the coming of Anti-Christ; though he took care to keep himself from contamination by saying that he had never looked into the book nor would he do so.[48] From a friar of opposite views, Luther, who had at first approved the publication of the work, soon came appreciation qualified by doubts about the competence and validity of his interpretation of Scripture: 'Erasmus has performed the task to which he was called, he has reinstated the ancient languages and recalled them from pagan studies. Perhaps like Moses he will die in the land of Moab, for he is powerless to guide men to those higher studies which lead to divine blessedness. I should very much like him to stop expounding the Scriptures for he is not equal to the task.'[49] Here Luther plainly does not consider that Erasmus has provided an effective theological exposition of the New Testament in his annotations: as was shown above, Erasmus produced them in the form and style of his commentary in his *Adagia* and had affirmed that they were not intended as theological exegesis. This distinguishing of emphasis and purpose between the two men marks the watershed between Erasmus on the one hand and developing Protestantism and the theological counter-attack by reforming Catholicism on the other. Erasmus deliberately intended to limit theological controversy: he would accept that the new theology written by the Lutherans was better written than that of the scholastics and less swaddled in syllogisms, but nevertheless he saw it as a dogmatic theology, though now wholly grounded on the Scriptures and the Fathers; and dogmatic theology on any basis, scholastic or Biblical, Erasmus believed to be a turning away from the simplicity of the teaching of Christ and His apostles. That Erasmus like the Protestant Luther and like the Catholic Contarini was a religious reformer who deeply desired newness of life in the Church should not need to be emphasized—it is the major reason for his editing, translating and annotating the Greek New Testament.[50]

Erasmus the Reformer turned away from all the institutional aspects of the Church and the secularized nature of its Curial control which was diffused throughout the hierarchy and based upon the complexities of canon law, a legal system loathed by the humanist jurisconsults who admired Erasmus. He instinctively responded to the sympathy of so many of the best informed laymen of his time as well as of those clergy sympathetic to the new trilingual studies, who desired the renewal of a piety which did not rely on mere sacramentalism, so formalized by this time; or on preaching farced with irrelevant if entertaining stories from the legends of saints; or on theologians who were the swordsmen of dialectics rather than guides to Christ's people. He tried to turn men away from these false directions to another path which he described in a phrase which could be misunderstood today, 'philosophia Christi', for it did not mean an elaborate intellectual structure but a living relationship with Christ. Here he showed his debt (not readily acknowledged by him) to the spirit of the *Devotio moderna*, seen at its noblest in the *De Imitatione Christi* of Thomas à Kempis, and the environment of his youth among the Brethren of the Common Life; to the insistence of Colet on the freshness of the new Biblical studies of the New Testament in Greek; and to his reading of Origen who showed him how piety and learning could expound the Scriptures without the wearisome distinctions of scholastic exegesis, or the earnest but narrow efforts of the greatest of medieval exegetes, Nicholas of Lyra. Erasmus knew better than Luther the courts of princes and the households of prelates, the secularized intrigues of the Curia and the ramifications of that spirit throughout the hierarchy in Christendom. He knew that formalized sacramentalism could not be a substitute for an inward piety transforming life; he knew that Scripture must be the source and goal of all sound theology, and that faith was trust in God and not merely the things to be believed in order to avoid heresy. But he saw no advantage in rending the visible church asunder nor, in order to reform it, in insisting on the centrality and concentrated force of the Augustinian doctrine of grace with its emphasis on man's depravity, loss of freewill to do good in God's sight, the consequent irrelevance of good works as conducing to salvation, and its impassioned assertion of prevenient grace. That his own alternative was possible in the situation of the times; that Luther was right in the end because he went to the root of the matter; and that Erasmus was too donnish and literary, will always be arguable: but that Erasmus had a consistent position as a Reformer and as an advocate of renewed Christian faith and life, that he was not merely an ambitious literary man who used these themes to attract notice, beat down his enemies, and find the favour of the fashionable and powerful, can be demonstrated.

With undeniable integrity and often real courage in face of

positive danger, Erasmus expounded, allusively in ironies like *Moriae Encomium*; directly in serious writings on religion like the *Enchiridion Militis Christianae*; more discursively in his *Adagia*, *Colloquia*, and *Querela Pacis*; and supremely concentrated in the prefaces, as well as to a less degree in the Annotations to his edition of the New Testament, and his *Paraphrases* (summing up in themselves the Erasmian style of religion and piety) a way of religious renewal which he hoped would indirectly affect the administration, worship and theology of the Church and more directly influence the daily lives of Christian men and women. He did not explicitly call for alteration in the institutions of the Church, in the papacy and the hierarchy, nor did he call for radical changes in the sacramental system so important for the institutional Church, but he did undermine some of these walls of largely medieval construction although he thought of himself as proposing no more than themes of renewal. In Spain, Italy and England especially, and also in France and Germany, the Erasmians were prominent men and most of them conceived of Church reform along lines indicated by Erasmus. It would be difficult to define the range and quality of the influence of Erasmus on so many men in the first half of the sixteenth century in matters of religious reform, though the task is not impossible as the example of *Erasme et l'Espagne* by M. Bataillon shows in a thorough examination of this influence in one country. That this influence was not only literary can be seen in the possibility that the Henrician Reformation in England was not merely an arbitrary rejection of the papacy in favour of a brutal Royal Supremacy as many saw the changes under Henry VIII (including Luther and Calvin as well as Catholic observers), but as capable of description on Erasmian lines, although Erasmus himself would have disapproved of the schism. The main decisions could be paralleled in his writings: the turning to the Christian Prince (Charles V, Francis I, Henry VIII) for initiative in Church reform where the papacy seemed powerless or unwilling to do so; the abolition of the religious life in monasteries and nunneries would seem little loss to Erasmus the detractor of monks; nor would the cutting down of too many Saints' Days which led the people into idleness and, worse, half-secularized religion, have lacked his approval; the abolition of centres of superstitious concern for relics at the shrines would find support from Erasmus' ironically contemptuous account of the visit of

Colet and himself to the shrine of St Thomas of Canterbury; the publishing of the Bible in English had the backing of his assertions on the value of vernacular versions of the Scriptures; the support by Henry for a trilingual college at Oxford and his appointing of professorships in the biblical languages shows his approval of that New Learning which Erasmus made it a great part of his life's work to promote. It is equally significant that Henry, whose accession had delighted the humanists of Europe, was an admirer of men of the New Learning, praised Erasmus to Charles V and Leo X and gave him other excuses for boasting of this royal flattery. It was tragic for his hopes that Erasmus lived to hear of Henry's judicial murder of Sir Thomas More whom he regarded as an exemplar of the 'philosophia Christi', and whose desire for Church reform (which did not weaken his rejection of schism) he would have preferred to the confident Protestantism of Ulrich Zwingli or the sectarianism of Hans Denck, though both were strongly Erasmian in their beginnings.

The essential theme of the 'philosophia Christi', as has been seen above, was marked by the anti-scholastic, anti-dogmatic and anti-speculative habit of mind and by a marked distrust of, if not positive rejection of, much of the theology of the Schools whether Thomist, Scotist or Occamist. It meant concentrating not upon the wide range of dogmas and the philosophical analysis and defence of them, but upon the limitation of the number of dogmas and upon them being clearly shown to be scriptural in origin; and turning away from over-emphasis on the sacramental system as well as from the debate on grace involving the grim labyrinth of antinomies on predestination and freewill, foreknowledge and meritorious works. Here Erasmus showed his aversion to the way the debates of late scholasticism on the doctrines of the sacraments and of grace helped to evolve the divisions between Catholics and Protestants. Against formalism and rigidity, Erasmus insisted on those things which made for Christian freedom in the gospel. For him the method of Church reform lay not in vigorous attacks on merit, on clerical abuses, and on the papacy, but on a slow process of self-knowledge and self-improvement by members of the Church led by gentle persuasion. Its foundation was the Bible, more especially the New Testament with its teachings made as practicable and intelligible as would be consistent with loyalty to the text; and to achieve this end, more would be gained by studying classical authors and the patristic Biblical exegetes like Jerome and Origen than from becoming entangled in the nets of scholastic interpretations of the fourfold sense of Scripture. All was to be focused on piety of mind and heart gained through the personal conviction and effort of the believer, who should not rely alone on the external rites of the Church since these were by comparison with Scripture poor conductors of spiritual insight. The life of virtue should be the product of the 'philosophia Christi' shown especially in loving kindness: the traditionalist assertors of dogmatic rectitude seemed to Erasmus to be men of worldly power rather than followers of Christ. Again and again Erasmus returned to the theme of Christian love which was also the drive behind his passionate detestation of war with its hatreds, its cruelties, and its mindless destruction. The *Querela Pacis* is only one instance of his writings on this theme, and it was his love for peace and charity which drew him away from schism or Protestantism in Christendom.

Erasmus set forth plainly the meaning of the 'philosophia Christi' in the *Paraclesis* placed before his edition of the New Testament and less directly in its companion little treatise the *Ratio seu Methodus compendio perveniendi ad veram theologiam*. The sub-heading of the *Paraclesis* is 'Exhortation to the study of the Christian Philosophy' and the phrase occurs fourteen times set out in the pattern of rhetorical exhortation renewed by the humanists of the time, for 'eloquence' was one of the driving forces of the early sixteenth century and Erasmus used it to call men of good-will concerned for this ideal of the Christian life to seek a nobler eloquence than Cicero because more effective if not so elegant. (Erasmus disliked Ciceronianism not only because of its tendency to artificiality but also because of its use as a papal instrument of diplomacy.) The preconditions of this philosophy of Christ are the spirit of piety and gentleness, and a pure and simple faith in the Word of God; and these can be found not only among the great ones of the world and the educated, but also among simple folk and it is found in manner of life rather than in argument and debate.

I am not at all in agreement with those who wish to prevent the Holy Scripture being read by the unlearned and translated into popular speech, as if Christ had taught things so complicated that scarcely a handful of theologians could understand them, or as if the Christian religion had no other defence than ignorance. . . . This kind of philosophy rests upon the feelings more than upon syllogisms, it is rather life than discussion, rather inspiration than erudition and rather conversion than reasoning. . . . If it is reserved for some to become learned men it is not forbidden to anyone to be Christian, to nobody to have faith, I would even boldly say, to no one to become a theologian. . . . The philosophy of Christ, which calls itself a rebirth, is it in fact any other thing than the restoration of a nature which had been created good? . . . The goal is to follow the pattern of Jesus Christ: the rules of religious orders or teachings of theological Schools are not necessary to understanding the simplicity of the teaching of Christ and His apostles: Christ is the way of life, the goal of mankind's endeavour and he is found uniquely in the New Testament. He said: 'If you love me, keep my word'.[51]

That Erasmus was a forerunner of both textual and historical criticism of the Bible is true but subsidiary to his ultimate purpose of the transformation of European society by men of good-will following the teaching of Christ and His apostles.[52] Since this by-passed so much of what the medieval Church had built up to provide salvation for men, was Erasmus proposing an alternative version of the Church? Catholic historians in our time like Joseph Lortz and Hubert Jedin see him as undermining and betraying Catholicism: for Lortz he was as serious a danger as Luther. In his own time he was accused of heresy by ardent traditionalists at the faculties of theology at Paris and Louvain, but these judgments were and are excessive. The position of Lortz and Jedin rests upon a view of Catholicism repristinated at the Council of Trent and which was not clearly expressed in Erasmus' lifetime, and is now under serious challenge in the theological situation arising from the Council of the Vatican II. Those of his Catholic contemporaries who opposed him were narrow and uninspired in outlook, nor did their judgment commend itself to men like More and Contarini whose loyalty to the Catholic Church should be beyond dispute. Did the admiration of Bucer, Zwingli and Oecolampadius and that of the Edwardine Protestants who caused the English version of Erasmus' *Paraphrases* to be set up in the parish churches of England, mean that he was a Protestant in all but name? Men would not forget that he died at Basel in a city brought into Protestantism by his disciple Oecolampadius.

He certainly had in common with the Protestant Reformers their great principles of appeal to the Scriptures as the source of theological truth and Christian life, of insisting on the Church being seen as the congregation of faithful men and women, the Corpus Mysticum, and turning away from the juridical and legalistic aspects of the Church's institutions; of turning away from the view of the sacraments as being of themselves the instruments of salvation, to emphasize two or three of them and this with intense concern for their spiritual reality. He could even write of justification by faith as in his Paraphrase of *Romans* I. 13 'Evangelium autem voco justificationem per fidem in Jesum Christum filium Dei quem lex promisit et praefiguravit': although he saw no need for the revolutionary force which Luther put into the concept. But Erasmus had no use for religion that struck like a thunderclap, and Calvin's insistence on all things being brought in subjection to the sovereignty of God would have seemed to him as a potential distortion of the simplicities of faith. It is true that observers of insight deeply involved in the spiritual crisis of the time like Albrecht Dürer saw in Erasmus in 1521, on a false rumour of Luther's death, Luther's successor in the struggle against the abuses of the Roman Church. But that was in 1521; Erasmus had not then finally committed himself against Luther: that was to come three years later in his *De Libero Arbitrio*. Did the Protestants feel like Browning on Wordsworth:

'Just for a handful of silver he left us,
    Just for a ribbon to stick in his coat?'

From the outsider's viewpoint, Erasmus died rich and there was a persistent rumour that the Pope had offered him high status if he remained a Catholic (though Erasmus did not in fact allow himself to be compromised in this way). But Erasmus never really shared the Protestant experience of grace; the agony of Luther's struggle like the 'subita conversio' of Calvin were not for him. His energies were dying when the Protestants began to flourish, and their insistence on schism deeply disturbed him.

Erasmus belonged to an earlier generation, to the men of the golden age of Northern Christian humanism 1490–1530, who believed in amelioration and never dreamed of schism or of rival orthodoxies vying in bitterness with the diatribes in that Scholasticism which they thought they had overcome. By the Diet of Worms, 1521, Luther's revolution was under way, and Europe was going to be rent asunder after the Diet of Augsburg in 1530.

Erasmus' reform failed in his hopes for it in his lifetime through forces which he had not foreseen though its inspiration was never lost: the followers of Melanchthon shared many of his principles, Erasmus' fellow-countryman Hugo Grotius was a new Erasmus for his time, and the Church of England has never forgotten wholly its Erasmian beginnings—for did not Hooker face Puritanism with certain weapons used by Erasmus? How many of the interests of reform Catholicism in our time after Vatican II revive, even if unconsciously, his aspirations for his Church?

NOTES

[1] *Essays by the late Mark Pattison*, ed. H. Nettleship, Oxford, 1889, vol. I. 79.

[2] *Opus Epistolarum Des. Erasmi Roterodami*, ed. P. S. Allen, vol. II. 420.

[3] *Desiderii Erasmi Roterodami Opera Omnia*, Leyden, 1703, I. 1001 E.

[4] Allen, *op. cit.*, I. 103.

[5] Allen, *op. cit.*, I. 332.

[6] Allen, *op. cit.*, I. 328.

[7] *Hieronymi Opera Omnia*, Paris, Chevallon, 1533. Prefatory letter to Archbishop Warham, 1524. Also in Allen, *op. cit.*, II. 220.

[8] Allen, *op. cit.*, I. 115.

[9] Allen, *op. cit.*, I. 410.

[10] Allen, *op. cit.*, I. 412.

[11] Allen, *op. cit.*, IX. 370.

[12] *Erasmi Opuscula*, ed. W. K. Ferguson, The Hague, 1933, 136.

[13] Ferguson, *op. cit.*, 141.

[14] Ferguson, *op. cit.*, 145.

[15] Ferguson, *op. cit.*, 178.

[16] Ferguson, *op. cit.*, 179.

[17] Ferguson, *op. cit.*, 190.

[18] Allen, *op. cit.*, I. 288.

[19] Allen, *op. cit.*, I. 305.

[20] Allen, *op. cit.*, I. 7.

[21] Allen, *op. cit.*, I. 352 (50 is the Vulgate number of the Psalm).

[22] Allen, *op. cit.*, I. 381.

[23] Allen, *op. cit.*, I. 405.

[24] Allen, *op. cit.*, II. 77.

[25] *Hieronymi Opera Omnia*, Paris, Chevallon, 1533, vol. I. 3 vs. Also in Allen, *op. cit.*, II. 218.

[26] Allen, *op. cit.*, III. 96.

[27] Allen, *op. cit.*, 182–3 for P. S. Allen's account of Erasmus' preparations for his New Testament.

[28] Allen, *op. cit.*, II. 4.

[29] Allen, *op. cit.*, II. 253.

30 Allen, *op. cit.*, II. 182.

31 Allen, *op. cit.*, I; to Gilles 517, to Rogerius 570.

32 Allen, *op. cit.*, II. 23.

33 Allen, *op. cit.*, II. 78.

34 Allen, *op. cit.*, II. 253.

35 F. H. A. Scrivener, *A Plain Introduction to the Criticism of the New Testament*, 4th ed., 1894, vol. II. 185.

36 Allen, *op. cit.*, II. 226 and 248.

37 John Foxe, *Actes and Monuments*, ed. J. Pratt, 4th ed., n.d., vol IV, 635.

38 Allen, *op. cit.*, I. 418.

39 Allen, *op. cit.*, III. 381.

40 *Desiderii Erasmi Roterodami Opera Omnia*, Leyden, 1703, VII. *In Annotationes Novi Testamenti Praefatio.*

41 Allen, *op. cit.*, II. 315.

42 *Novi Testamenti Annotationes*, ed. 1519, Matt. XXIII, 5.

43 Allen, *op. cit.*, IV. 310.

44 *Ibid.*, IV, 11

45 *Annotationū Libri duo alter in annotatiões prioris aeditionis novi testamenti Desiderii Erasmi alter in annotatiões posterioris aeditiõis eiusdē*, Louvain, 1520. On the lack of basis in the Greek text for the Latin translation, sig. DDiii. For the verses at the end of *Revelation* provided by Erasmus, Fo. LXXXVII. 'Nam si grēca bene habent: cur emendatur? sin male: cur tantopere tibi placet: secundum ea: nostra mutare: reijicere: damnare?'

46 A. Bludau, *Die beiden ersten Erasmus-Ausgaben des N.T. (Biblische Studien*, VII. Band, 5. Heft), Freiburg im Breisgau, 1902. Here is given a full account of the controversies which arose over the publication of the first two editions.

47 Allen, *op. cit.*

48 Allen, *op. cit.*, IV. 556.

49 *D. Martin Luthers Werke: Kritische Gesamtausgabe; Briefwechsel*, Weimar, 1933, 3 Band, 96.

50 In his Colloquy entitled *Peregrinatio religionis ergo*, 1526, there are foreshadowed many changes about to take place in England on the subject of images, relics, and pilgrimages.

51 *Opera Omnia, op. cit.*, Tome VI.

52 There is not space, nor is this the place, to deal with Erasmus' other writings on Scriptural subjects: his expositions of the Psalms, his *Paraphrases*, and his writings on the principles of Hermeneutics, nor to draw attention to his attitude to the Old Testament and his use of allegorizing. Both on his Biblical scholarship and on his aims as a Reformer of the Church there is given here no more than essentials.

V

The Latinity of Erasmus

D. F. S. THOMSON

Style

ERASMUS has so often been taxed with the sin of journalism, which may be presumed to imply slipshod and ephemeral composition, that it is easy to forget the very high regard in which he was held both as a poet (in the Renaissance interpretation of the term) and as a writer of Latin prose, by the men of his own day. For them it was precisely his admirable and distinctive manner of writing that arrested attention and caused him to be compared with Petrarch—by the few who still read Petrarch then[1]—or more frequently perhaps with Poggio or Politian. The Latin he wrote so rapidly and so easily was an idiom he had created, in a medium he had mastered. If he rarely blotted a line or even, by his own confession, a letter, this was simply because, in a sense hardly conceivable to most of the learned in his age, he wrote as he talked and inwardly thought.[2]

Accomplished practitioners of literary Latin in that period too frequently composed as from the study, at one or more removes from the point at which words and feelings met in daily experience. Erasmus, on the other hand, although (and perhaps because) he commanded at will the expressive resources not of Cicero or Livy but of the entire language, saw no reason to assume as his own the linguistic inclinations of any ancient Roman. His was a true *Sprachgefühl*, acquired (not without tedious labour) over those lonely years of boyhood when, his energetic mind turned bookward for want of living intellects with which to communicate, he devoured Terence and the other Latin classics of style. Since his range of reading was matched by his memory and absorptive capacity and a certain relish for words, this time of quiet study had for result a personal kind of Latinity—eclectic, inclined to the usages of later periods, yet unmistakably his own.

That Erasmus began his literary career, and made his reputation, as a poet, not as a writer of prose, might be guessed from his choice of language, especially of epithets, as when (Allen 9.436) he writes of Basil's *flexanima eloquentia*. But it shows in his prose style also; phrases like *ne roga, sum facilis dare*, betray the syntax of poetry. Moreover, Erasmus is not prone to use abstract argumentation, even on theological subjects; he loves the concrete fact, the visual image, and he loves to tell a tale. On the whole his sentences avoid periodic structure and rhetorical climax, though he could handle these with effortless mastery and with complete clarity when he chose to do so. He much prefers to present a topic in short statements that succeed and illuminate one another in turn. From this point of view the department of *copia verborum* that is concerned with *synonyms* assumes the greatest importance. Each word having overtones of which Erasmus is fully conscious, parallel statement of a theme in this way results often in a deeper insight into the situation presented than could be obtained by using a developed argument and a fully consistent set of terms. The adage and the cliché, to which he is able to lend revivifying power, also serve him well here; by their ancient, succinct wisdom he takes short cuts in the development of a thought, while at the same time adorning it. At the same time, as a good Renaissance 'orator' should, he exploits whenever necessary the whole traditional apparatus of devices furnished by rhetoric: repetition of words, antithesis of ideas, increasing length of clauses. But he will often break the monotony of the more laborious periods by ellipses, asyndeton, anacoluthon,[3] trusting much to the intelligence of his reader. His aim is to show, to tell, not to hammer a point home by logical argument; to exemplify, rather than to prove.

If his mastery of the entire resources of Latin was not wholly unconscious, it was at least not self-conscious. Such an absorption of the medium into the roots of his being at an early and impressionable age conferred, as we have seen, a rapidity which brought it about that even 'his Greek Testament, like everything else that he did, was done in a hurry',[4] and at the same time distinguished him on the one hand from the more studied Ciceronians, among whom in his day were Budé, Longolius and Scaliger,[5] and on the other hand from the practitioners of a less distinguished, not seldom a little incorrect Latinity, such as Colet.

It may be worth while for a moment to try to fix his position in the annals of Latin style. He is clearly above the clumsy attempts at wit of the *Epistolae Obscurorum Virorum*; his effects are less contrived than those of Longolius, or of Budé for that matter, and of this he is aware; he has, like his friend and disciple Beatus Rhenanus, a great deal of charm, but the more sparkling and contagious charm, allied with swiftness and extemporaneity, belongs to Erasmus. A minute piece of practical criticism may help to show the difference. Certain editions of More's *Utopia* print an introductory letter to that work, addressed to Lupset by Guillaume Budé. The vocabulary in this letter is strikingly similar to that of a letter or dialogue by Erasmus: it includes the post-classical word *nullibi*, used by Vitruvius; the Greek importation *scopus*, 'aim', a favourite of Erasmus; *impostura*, another Erasmian favourite; and phrases like *in praecipitium* which Erasmus would not have scorned. There are one or two legal terms, belonging to a jargon which Erasmus does not much affect.[6] But when Budé proceeds to speak of a woman as *culinaria dispensatrix*, and crowns it with the phrase *omnis cura census ampliatrix*; when, in order to say 'build up a fortune', he has to excogitate the expression *penates suos architectari*, to which a few lines later he adds *civitatem architectari*;[7] when a simple letter is *epistola internuntia*, and the intervening spaces, which are not large, are filled up with rococo adornments of language (*excipulae, planicae improbitates*), we feel ourselves to be in a realm of affectation to which Erasmus is a stranger.

The contrast with More, vastly less severe, is nevertheless instructive. In the year 1507, some of the *Dialogues* of Lucian were translated from Greek into Latin, partly by More, mainly by Erasmus. There is a difference between the two versions. Where More is periodic and stately, Erasmus is lively and direct; he comes, as Allen puts it, halfway to meet the reader. The *Utopia*, again, together with most of More's writings, employs the Classical periodic sentence with its calculated sinuosities and often complex subordination of clauses. Erasmus seldom constructs his Latin thus; instead he uses parallel or consecutive statement, and for this reason seems freer and more natural. Many things he and More had in common: wit, a pronounced taste for diminutive forms of words, a preference, amounting to a love, for dialogue.

In vocabulary, there is much resemblance between them. But Erasmus scores with his infectious rapidity and off-hand discursiveness. He is also simpler, less whimsical, less peculiar and more respectful of tradition in his choice of words.[8] Even when he does write in periodic sentences, these themselves do not demand the active attention of the reader in the same way as those of More or of Cicero. 'Les gageures de la période ont disparu. Les idées se succèdent exactement dans l'ordre que nous attendions.'[9] In a word, Erasmus writes as a modern man.

Considered purely as a Latinist, Colet stands somewhere near the other end of the spectrum from those we have been discussing. A fair picture of his qualities and limitations appears in the long letter, part of which Erasmus devoted to the Life of Colet:

> Recte loquendi copiam non ferebat peti e praeceptionibus grammaticorum, quas asseverabat officere ad bene dicendum, nec id contingere nisi evolvendis optimis auctoribus; sed huius opinionis ipse poenas dedit. Cum enim esset et natura et eruditione facundus, ac dicenti mira suppeteret orationis ubertas, tamen scribens subinde labebatur in his quae solent notare critici. Atque hac, ni fallor, gratia a libris scribendis abstinebat, atque utinam non abstinuisset: nam huius viri cogitationes quacunque etiam lingua proditas optarim.[10]

> He would not allow that the proper place to look for a treasury of correct diction lay in the grammarian's rules; for these, he said, hindered the acquisition of a good style, the latter being something that resulted exclusively from the diligent study of the best authors. But he paid a price for maintaining this point of view; for though he was eloquent both by natural disposition and by training, and had a remarkable degree of fluency in the spoken word, still when it came to writing he repeatedly made mistakes on points that critics habitually censure. And it was for this reason, if I am not mistaken, that he tended to refrain from writing books. I wish he had not done so; for this was a man whose thoughts I should have liked to see published in any kind of language at all.

Erasmus' Latinity (at least in prose; much of the surviving poetry should be considered as prentice work)[11] is on the whole very even in quality. This is not so say that he has only one manner of writing; there is great variety not only among the kinds, whether dialogue, letter, Biblical commentary or paraphrase, dedicatory epistle or educational treatise, but also among the individual works.[12] The *Antibarbarus*, for example, is a Ciceronian dialogue, infused with a gaiety and liveliness which Cicero never quite managed to confer on his own literary or philosophic dialogues (it is hardly germane to this brief enquiry to ask why Erasmus succeeded); the same may be said of the *Ciceronianus*. In the *De Conscribendis Epistolis*, with its intention to instruct, there is much Quintilian at the beginning, less perhaps later; on the other hand the *Querela Pacis*, belonging to an adult world, is somewhat Plinian in the character of its style. If the *Enchiridion* knows little Classical adornment save a few choice echoes of Horace's odes, and reveals a paucity of rare words taken from the ancient authors, the *Praise of Folly* shows quite the contrary phenomenon in the last respect, being crammed with verbal *trouvailles* from Erasmus' favourite reading as well as from the vocabulary of scholastic dialectic (which Erasmus is by no means loth to borrow) and clerical eloquence.

In those works where the author feels a pious obligation of gravity, classical influences are kept in check; as a result of this restraint, such works (the colloquy *Inquisitio de Fide*, for example) tend to lack stylistic distinction; thus, the *De sarcienda Ecclesiae concordia* receives its sober classical garnishing from a very few references to Horace; but when Erasmus' own feeling, in these compositions, rises to a sufficient height of engaged excitation, a fine austere eloquence results, as in the *Paraclesis* to the New Testament. And when he demits the entire responsibility of pastoral solemnity (whether exercised towards pious laymen or children) his range of verbal colour and allusion is extended almost to infinity; witness the later editions of the *Colloquies*, the private letters and many Adages. Invective, finally, may remove restraints in another way; and for this reason the *Spongia adversus Hutteni aspergines* contains some of his most effective and trenchant prose. Yet the phenomena attending Erasmus' mode, or modes, of expression amount to no more than the permissible manifestations of succeeding concerns and emotions on the face of one who handled the Latin language always with authority. One can hardly help observing how very faithfully the adage here fits: *le style, c'est l'homme même*.

Those who have best understood the relation between Erasmus the man and his style have always placed their finger on the rapidity and extemporaneity of composition which is the key to so much in him. This, with engaging humility, he himself recognized as a fault; but also explained and in part defended, in passages like the following:

> Natura sum extemporalis et ad recognitionem mire piger. Et scis quam difficile sit pugnare cum natura. . . . Neque illa M. Tullii myrothecia conueniunt iis qui ad docendum parati sunt uel religionis negotium tractant. . . . Mystica postulant siccum quoddam dictionis genus. . . .[13]

> By nature I am both inclined to extemporize, and extraordinarily loth to revise; and you know how hard it is to fight against one's nature. . . . Also, the famed beauties of Cicero's style are not suited to the needs of those who are connected with the conduct of education or involved in the business of the Church. . . . Religious topics call in fact for an austere kind of style. . . .'

The presence of the same extempore quality in his poetry too is admitted in some of Erasmus' letters (for example Nos 112 and 113 in Allen's edition); and the letters themselves often conclude with the significant adverb *tumultuarie*, 'in a tearing hurry'. Beatus Rhenanus, the intimate friend of Erasmus' later years, says of him: 'Ipse stilum apertum, extemporalem, purum, facilem et argutum semper amavit.'[14] 'He himself always clung to an informal, extemporaneous, clear, simple and explicit style.' When he half-humorously included himself as a character in his *Ciceronianus*, Erasmus put his finger on his own penchant for haste: 'Praecipitat omnia.' 'He dashes everything off in a hurry', he observes in self-description.[15] It is true—and of some interest— that he shared this quality with Thomas More, who (thinking chiefly of himself) speaks of his own Hythloday's style as *subitarius atque extemporalis*. But Erasmus' easy rapidity differs first in degree and then in kind from More's: as I have suggested, it carries him into a modernity of feeling never quite achieved by his friend's more studied Latin. P. S. Allen remarks:

> It is interesting to compare the rough drafts of Erasmus' letters with those of his correspondents. . . . With Erasmus . . . the lines flow swiftly over the page, true and even, with hardly a word corrected. . . . Many of his controversial works are veritable *tours de force*, dashed off in a few days. . . . This headlong trait in his character. . . . There was no time to halt for verification of details. . . . He had no time to spare for attaining precision. . . . His work was always done in heat. . . . He read, he wrote, *tumultuarie*, *praecipitanter*. When he had formed a design, he liked to carry it out *uno impetu*.[16]

And yet for all this speed, Erasmus' Latin is clearly better than that of Colet for example, which is workmanlike but, as has just been shown, uneasy; in places, Erasmus himself shows how conscious he is of Colet's stylistic weakness and proneness to error, and hesitates, where Colet had felt no hesitation, to recommend the reading of certain Christian writings, the diction of which was of dubious correctness.[17] Erasmus has reservations too about Petrarch: great and important, but to be praised more for his intentions than for his accomplishments, at any rate in Latin. With Erasmus it was inevitable, given the speed of composition which was a part of his nature, and the state of fatigue in which a certain proportion of his daily task was always accomplished, that at times he should lose track of a long sequence of clauses and change, for example, the mood of a verb. Indeed the eyebrows of a less than sympathetic scholar who came to a page—any page—of Erasmus, in prose or in verse, fresh from the ancient classics would not remain for long unraised. But, in Mark Pattison's[18] words: 'He *spoiled* nothing by anxious revision in terror lest some phrase not of the golden age should escape from his pen. He confesses apologetically to Christopher Longolius (Ep. iii. 63; 402) that it was his habit to extemporize all he wrote, and that this habit was incorrigible; "effundo uerius quam scribo omnia".' The best commentary on Pattison's word 'spoiled' is perhaps Erasmus' description of the stylistic purists: 'Grave flagitium esse clamitant, si verbum ullum misceatur Epistolae, quod legentem vel tantisper remoretur.'[19] 'They raise cries of Outrage! on every occasion when a letter contains any word that, even for a moment, delays the reader's eye.' Typical of the earliest generation of hostile critics was Scaliger, who 'thought Erasmus would have done better if he had kept more closely to the classical models'. Yet even Scaliger praised the Latinity of Erasmus in comparison with that of Jerome; while Erasmus with characteristic modesty regretted merely that too much familiarity with Jerome was the cause of a lack of stylistic purity in his own Latin.

The question of Erasmus' attitude to puristic 'Ciceronianism' must be briefly discussed at this point. On the one hand, Erasmus has strong views about a truly *correct* Latin style and the means of attaining it: not only in the *De Ratione Studii* (I. 521 D) does he suggest a method of imbibing and imitating classical Latinity by reading the best ancient authors (beginning with Terence and

Plautus, and of course including Cicero and Caesar, as well as Sallust, Horace and Virgil), but in the dialogue *Ciceronianus* he gives a series of quick, clever assessments of hundreds of Latin styles and their authors ancient, medieval and modern, tested by success in approaching, if not actually reaching, what Erasmus himself considers a genuinely Ciceronian level. Incidentally, he exhibits *en route* his own almost incredible breadth of reading. In the course of this 'de claris oratoribus', so to call it, he takes occasion to defend some of the pagan and patristic sources he liked to draw upon in order to possess the huge vocabulary that seemed to him necessary to the vitality of Latin considered as a living speech—Aulus Gellius, about whose *phrasis affectata et verborum copia paene superfluens* Nosoponus (invented to represent purism) grumbles (1007 A); and in modern times Pontanus, who is unpopular because he uses a myriad of non-Ciceronian words (1019 F). As for the purists, 'Ciceronianos sese vocant, intolerabili supercilio reiicientes omnium scripta quae Ciceronis lineamenta non referunt: et adolescentiam a ceterorum scriptorum lectione deterritam ad unius M. Tullii superstitiosam aemulationem adigunt.' (971). And he points to their real weakness and superficiality. They believe themselves to be truly Ciceronian if they begin a periodic sentence with *quamquam* or *etsi* or *cum* or *si*! (986 B). As for himself, Erasmus makes it clear that he is prepared to exploit the entire resources of the language as it has historically been developed, in any save barbarous hands, up to and including those of scholastic philosophy and the currency of his own time in its daily affairs (an aspect of Erasmus' Latinity that editors have hardly as yet sufficiently emphasized): 'Ne affectat quidem Tulliano more dicere, non abstinens a vocibus theologis, interim ne a sordidis quidem.' (1013 F.) But where Erasmus borrowed or even invented, he did so in accordance with the genius of the language as the best writers handled it; and here, if anywhere, his true accomplishment as a Latinist stood revealed.

Some critics, for example Remy and Dunil-Marquebreucq in their edition of *Dulce bellum inexpertis* (p. 14), have spoken of Erasmus' 'souci de déplaire' in choosing non-Ciceronian words as if by preference, on purpose to spite the purists, 'parce qu'ils feront grincer les dents des cicéroniens'. This is slightly exaggerated. Indeed, if such a claim were entertained, it might lead to the belief that this was the cause of the famous outcry against the *Ciceronianus*, which has caught the attention of Erasmus' biographers and which certainly gave him much trouble; whereas in fact the reason lay in the omission of some scholars from Erasmus' long list, and the inclusion of others in what they considered unsuitable company, as for example the juxtaposition of the name of Guillaume Budé with that of the Paris printer Jodocus Badius, that led to the feuds: offended vanity being therefore the principal cause.

The attitude of Erasmus was really determined by his anxious desire to preserve Latin as a living, useful and flexible tongue and his belief that the material provided by the past as a whole should be made available, by adaptation if necessary, for the needs of the present. To give an example of his procedure: in the *Praise of Folly* (ed. J. B. Kan, p. 99) he takes the word *prorogator* from a very late author, namely Cassiodorus, but uses it in a manner that, while legitimately Latin, cannot be paralleled in Cassiodorus himself. Yet if he does sometimes find that the words which best, or most concisely, express his meaning are medieval ones, still on other occasions he is at pains to correct the medieval vocabulary when this seems imprecise or there exists a classical term as good or better. An instance of this is given by the changes he makes in course of revising the *Antibarbarus*, where he alters *saeculares* to *liberales* (*disciplinae*) twice, to *humanae* once, to *profanae* once (A. Hyma, *The Youth of Erasmus* pp. 286, 294, 304); again, *saeculares literae* to *ethnicae literae* (*ibid.*, p. 330), *gentiles* to *ethnici* (*ibid.*, pp. 313, 323, 329) and elsewhere to *profani* (*ibid.*, p. 329), and *farcinatoribus* to *agricolis* (*ibid.*, p. 319).

If he himself was a Ciceronian—as he was, in the sense that he exalted Cicero as the supreme master of literary style in the various kinds of prose[20]—then it was not by grace of any publication like Nizolius' *clavis Ciceroniana*[21] that such he became and remained. His range of vocabulary, which is truly extraordinary, and marks him out among even the great Humanists, far exceeds that of Cicero. But in another matter where he is supreme, and which represents perhaps the ultimate among his merits as a stylist, he proclaims himself a faithful pupil of his preceptor, namely in the *discrimination* of styles, especially in the epistolary *genre*. He has this in common with Petrarch; and in Petrarch's case the discovery of the Letters to Atticus had much to do with it. Yet when Erasmus turns from the private letter to the treatise or the dialogue he extends the same sensitivity to appropriate style and tone into each of the literary varieties he explores. In religious treatises his language, more than the subject itself dictates, betrays a heavy infusion of patristic Latinity, relieved by the sprightly digressions into personal anecdote that punctuate even the exegetical works, where it is much reduced. In educational writings he is straightforward and even, without syntactical complexity; as much as the letters, perhaps indeed more so, these essays give the feeling that they were composed *tumultuarie*. In the *Colloquies* he is for the most part unbuttoned, apt to play with words and to invent them. In the *Praise of Folly*, the style varies as the tone changes, from the familiar to that of an *ars contionandi*.

Language

Erasmus had a *penchant* for drafting into vigorous service odd and rare words borrowed from his favourite authors, who could be early or late, even patristic. In this matter he felt no pangs of conscience, resting serenely on the precept and example of his master Lorenzo Valla. If Valla had been ready to incur the hazard and the reality of an *Invectiva contra Vallam* from the pen of another great Humanist, because he deliberately on occasion preferred to bray with Apuleius rather than to speak with Cicero,[22] so was Erasmus. Many of the elements of language which he in this way resuscitated had made but a single appearance before, frequently in Plautus, in Persius or Juvenal, or in Aulus Gellius or Apuleius. When they appealed to his taste and seemed to him useful, he collected them, displayed them, and made them shine in use.

The taste for such serviceable curiosities was one of those he shared with Thomas More; and in the *Praise of Folly*, in whose title lurks the praise of More, they are present in a quite unusual proportion. The manner in which Erasmus employs them and the freedom and confidence with which he deploys them are the strongest testimony to the breadth of his reading among ancient Roman works of literature and the profundity of his knowledge of the language and grasp of its possibilities; for there was no thesaurus, no dictionary as yet, not even a Nizolius; and thus to reach out and grasp a word that had made a fleeting and unique appearance in a Plautine comedy (or in Macrobius, say, or Cassiodorus) and to confer upon it a second incarnation as the *mot juste* in a modern context, was to distance oneself at once from the *servum pecus* of all mere imitation and, in that sphere, to show the marks of creative genius.

Examples of such adaptation, which may be divided into Biblical, patristic and pagan in terms of their origin, occur everywhere in the corpus of his writings, though naturally in those of a religious complexion the Biblical and the patristic will be found to prevail. Among the list (merely a representative selection) which follows in order to illustrate this point will be found several of the expressions which, once adopted by Erasmus, became favourites and—perhaps inevitably, given the rapid and unrevising manner in which he composed—now and again show signs of overwork.

Taken from the Bible are, for example: *baiulare* (in a general sense for 'carry', replacing *portare*, *ferre* etc.); *colophizare*; *cophini* (for 'vessels'); *mammona*; *manducare* (in a general sense, replacing *edere*); *offendiculum* (derived probably from the Vulgate use, although it occurs in Pliny's letters); *praevaricator* ('sinner'), also *praevaricatio* and *praevaricari*; *romphaea*; *zizania* ('tares'; at least once treated as fem. singular). From patristic sources come the following: *cadaverosus*, *correptio* (for 'reproof'), *definitor*, *fruitio*, *ieiunatio*, *magnates*, *neomenia*, *pudescere*, *saginatus*, *signaculum*.

Rare words taken from pagan authors include these: *aqualicius*, *aspernabilis*, *balbuties*, *caecutiare*, *cantillare*, *congerro*, *consarcinare*, *dissertatio* ('disputation'), *edulis*, *fastidienter*, *figmentum*, *iactabundus*, *incogitantia*, *mulotriba*, *multiiugus*, *murmurare* ('complain', with its compounds), *nugamenta*, *obgannire*, *pensilis*, *peronatus*, *piamen*, *prorogator*, *protritus*, *repotia*, *subausterus*, *surrepticius*, *terricula*, *tusculum*, *unciola*.

Diminutives in Erasmus form a separate topic, inasmuch as their roots may lie in any of the three categories of linguistic innovation which we have mentioned, yet the results are formally indistinguishable. Often they are of regularly classical formation, but several degrees more frequent in occurrence than even a late Latin author would have permitted to himself.[23] (Erasmus himself remarks, 'Nec quia *scriptor* et *lectio* offendo apud Ciceronem, statim ausim dicere *scriptorculus* et *lectiuncula*'.)[24] The following list may be taken as representative (Margolin's edition of the *De Pueris Instituendis*, for which see the Bibliographical Note *infra*, gives a list of some forty diminutives to be found there): it will be observed that the list contains classical and Biblical words as well as those of Erasmian or at least Renaissance coinage:

Accessiuncula, adspersiuncula, aedificiolum, animula, annotatiuncula, apiculus ('tittle'), *aquula (consecrata), assentatiuncula, audaculus, avicula, cantiuncula, casula, cavillatiuncula, cervisiola, cibulum, ceremoniola, cessatiuncula, cogitatiuncula, colliculus, comoediola, commendatiunculus, compotatiuncula, conclusiuncula, confabulatiuncula, constitutiuncula, conventiculum, conviciolum, crassulus, crustulum, curiosuscule (disputari), cuticulam (curare), (de)ambulatiuncula, declaratiuncula, degustatiuncula, dictiuncula, dimicatiuncula, domuncula, facultatulae, feroculus, figulus, foliolum, fonticulus, formosulus, fortunula, fragmentulum, grandiusculus, guttula (vini), holusculum, horula, imaguncula, insulula, iuvenculus, labecula, laminula, leviculus, leunculus* (from *leo*), *lucernula, magistellus, mercedula, minusculum, minutulus, mitellus, monasteriolum, narratiuncula, nubecula, nummulus, obiectatiuncula, observatiuncula, oppidulum, oratiuncula, paullulus* (adj.), *pauperculus, pauxillulum, pecuniola, pensiculor, peregrinatiuncula, persuasiuncula, philosophastri, plantula, pluviola, portiuncula, potiuncula, praeceptiuncula, praemiolum, precatiuncula, precula, primitiolae, puellus, pugiunculus, pulvisculum, putidulus, quadrula, quaestiuncula, radiolus, ramusculus, religiosulus, rhetorculus, rosariola, rusculum, sacrificulus, salariolum, salutatiuncula, scintillula, scriniolum, scriptiuncula, signaculum, situla, sorbitiuncula, sphaerula, stellula, stultulus, suspiciosulus, tenebellus, terricula, testula, timidulus, traditiuncula, turricula, tusculum, unciola, veniola, verbulum, vexatiuncula, virguncula, voluptatula, vulnusculum, xeniola.*

The accumulation of diminutives is frequent, as in the phrases *infantuli testulam imbunt, stellulae flosculorum, parvula summula.* Sometimes a diminutive has a perfectly classical but not at first sight obvious sense: e.g. *amiculi,* 'close friends, cronies'; *religiosuli,* not 'slightly religious' but rather 'scrupulous about petty details'.

A complete list of those expressions of a somewhat striking character which recur again and again as one reads the works of Erasmus would no doubt furnish a valuable commentary on the preoccupations of his mind. A few of the most prominent among these favourites may be given:

Adglutino (with other compound forms of the same verb), *antelucanus, cantillare, cantio, cantiuncula, clancularius, combibones, compotatio, compotor, congerro, deliramentum, deliratio, digladiari, digladiatio, duntaxat* (meaning 'only', as in *Spongia adversus Hutteni aspergines*: 'non arbitror quemquam pontificem, duntaxat hunc...'), *emendicare, impostor, impostura, incunctanter, infrugiferus, magnates, praeceptio, precamen, precula, repullulascere, retrusius, technae* ('dodges, wiles'), *tragoedias excitare* ('make a fuss'), *ut est* (as in phrases like 'Episcopus, ut erat fervido ingenio . . .'), and finally nouns in *-trix*, for which Cicero himself had a weakness: e.g. *buccinatrix* (*Praise of Folly*, ed. J. B. Kan, p. 3), *comtrix* (*Opera Omnia* I 853 C), *concionatrix* (740 B), *deprecatrix* (740 B), *hortatrix* (adj.: 701 E), *ianitrix* (701 B), *lotrix* (844 C and 853 C), *textrix* (772 D), *tutrix* (539 A), *venditrix* (772 D), and so forth. (Utterly alien, however, to the Erasmian simplicity and straightforwardness is Guillaume Budé's contrived phrase *cura census ampliatrix*, with its studied artificiality: the contrast is instructive.)

A quiet relish for unusual words is shown in Erasmus' use of *fabulamenta, dapsilitas, obrudere, paenitentarius* (for 'confessor'), *magnificaticius* ('one who preaches on the Magnificat', his own invention of course, 851 A) and a variety of oddities patristic, medieval and modern. Sometimes he disapproves of a medievalism: at 692 A Erasmus writes *canonizavit*, but immediately adds 'sic etiam vocant'. In the *Antibarbarus*: 'poetice, quam poetriam vocare solent' [25]

The bubbling high spirits of Erasmus, and a vein of verbal fancy, led him sometimes to indulge in punning; and this, not only in the *Praise of Folly* (*Graeculi–graculi*) and the private letters (for example, *humanitas–immanitas*) but in every kind of composition. The serious work *De sarcienda ecclesiae concordia* provides a pun on *torcularia–torsit*; the educational treatises more than once play with the double meaning of *imperare liberis* ('children' or 'free men'); similarly, the *Enchiridion Militis Christiani* (10 D and 20 E) reveals the ambiguity in its own title's first word ('dagger' or 'handbook') as deliberate and conscious. The *Colloquies*, as might be expected, with their lively style, yield a rich harvest of Erasmian puns. That on *quoque* and *coque* in the colloquy *Confabulatio Pia* (692 E) comes from Cicero by way of Quintilian; but the others are original, even, regrettably, the outrageous double pun *natatilis beta–cacatilis bestia* in the *Synodus Grammaticorum* (824 F). Other puns in the *Colloquies* are these: *mores–mortes* (696 E), *camelus–Carmelita* (689 F), *apud Hibernos–hibernasti* (736 E), *lupos–lupas* (739 A), *observantes–observabo* (739 D), *prior–posterior* (a 'sub-Prior': 780 E), *cornix* in two senses (766 A), (Duns) *Scotus–σκότος* (746 F–747 A), *gratianus–gratiae* (784 C), *nuptiae Mortis cum Marte* (826 E), *pruriginosas–rubiginosas* (827 B), *podagra–'mentagra'* (827 C), *Cannius–een kanne* (833 F), *ἀχείρους–ἀχρείους* (836 A), *Merdardus* (for *Medardus*)–*merdosus* (851 D), *bella–bellaria* (864 D), *ambigere de finibus* (882 C), *sacer* (two meanings: 884 D); and the colloquy *Echo* is of course based on puns throughout. In the adage *Dulce Bellum Inexpertis* we may find, besides the pun or jingle *amori–amari* (and similarly *tum vincamus–cum vincemur*), word-play involving the proper names of Leo X (*agnus ad nocendum, leo rugiens adversus ea quae adversa sunt pietati*) and of the city of Florence (*Florentinorum civitas–florentissima*). In the *De Pronuntiatione* (913 B) good use is made (for the purposes of the dialogue) of a pun on *dominatus* and *domi natus*. A similar pun is found in more than one place on the name of Pope Clement: e.g. Allen 7.509f. (esp. 2059 ll. 6–7), *vidimus Clementem inclementissime tractatum*; cf. Allen 9.27, 170, 243 (esp. 2375 ll. 86–7; 2445 ll. 27–8; 2472 l. 36). The Life of Vitrarius contained in the famous letter to Jodocus Jonas contains a pun in its concluding phrase *habes vere gemmeum Vitrarium nostrum*. . . . The list might be still further enlarged. Nevertheless, for all his addiction to the practice of this form of wit, Erasmus has in mind for the most part, it would seem, his own reservation that decorum born of intellectual good manners must govern such sallies: *verum eorum qui liberales profitentur disciplinas, oportet et iocos esse liberales.*

The principle of *copia verborum*, as it was both preached and practised by Erasmus, excludes resort to modern vernaculars for the augmentation of Latin. The barbarism of the *agrestes linguae* was thus something external, which need be considered as neither an invasion of, nor a threat to, the integrity of the learned language; so long, at least, as it was kept in its proper place—outside. (By contrast, the late medieval jargon of *clerici* and *legulei* assumed in his eyes the aspect of a conspiracy against the well-being of Latin itself.) Only in the minutest number of instances is Erasmus compelled to include in his text a fragment of undigested German, let us say, in order to explain his meaning; *ut vulgo dicitur* is a phrase of the very rarest occurrence in his text,[26] and yet he of all writers in Latin, considering the vast and realistic canvas he painted and the inclination to narrative and anecdote that he brought to every kind of subject, might repeatedly have found reason to use it.

If, as happens now and then, help must be sought beyond Rome, he naturalizes at once the terms he borrows. *Bombarda* was already known as a Latin word for 'cannon'; it is so used in his *Spongia adversus Hutteni aspergines*, and in the *Colloquies*; a cannon-ball, therefore, becomes *sphaerula bombardica*. No ancient colour quite corresponds to the modern 'yellow'; so, when precisely this is required, Erasmus does not hesitate for once to latinize a German word, producing *gilvus* (690 F). A few of Erasmus' indulgences in a kind of modern Latin consist in borrowings from the Italianized diction of the earlier humanists: *abbreviatura, postilla*. A Wycliffite becomes *Viclevita* (783 F), a halberd is *halbardacha* (831 D, 833 B), and *stanneus* now means 'made of pewter' (688 E). But it is in the actual coinage of new words from Latin itself to meet utterly new needs that Erasmus shows himself to be most ingenious. Such are *perspicillum* for a 'spy-glass' or 'magnifying-glass' (780 E), *iusculum* (revived from Cato) for the kind of soup known as *minestra* (864 D), *conducticia mamma* for a professional wet-nurse (773 B) and *utricines* for bagpipers (827 A). It would be rash (until the distant day when a thesaurus of Renaissance Latin is taken in hand) to claim for any humanist the invention of a particular word; yet one cannot but feel confident that some at least among the following list, taken from a few representative works of Erasmus, were the children of his inventive brain:

(In prose) *amphibologiae, comptura, lucernarius, omnissimum* (after Plautus' *ipsissimum*), *utcumque permurmurare* ('gabble through any old how'), *polymachaeroplacides* (823 E), *praesulatus, pudicitas, urticetum* ('nettle bed'), *sesquihaereticus* (719 E), *sophistria, spiritosus*; perhaps *cyclopedia*.

(In verse) *flammivomus, ignivomus, moricanus, nymbriferus, organon* ('tongue'), *paranymphus, plasma, plastes, sophia*.

Many technical terms, principally medical or ecclesiastical in their reference, are borrowed by Erasmus from Greek and introduced into Latin for probably the first time in a number of cases; such are *malagma, myrothecia, Trias* for the Trinity, and there are many more.[27] A very favourite word in the Erasmian vocabulary is *scopus*, 'aim', though this Greek importation cannot be claimed as his own; Guillaume Budé has the same word in the same sense.[28] And a peculiar touch of Greek style in the Latin of Erasmus is to be found in expressions such as *mea de illo aestimatio*, a phrase we encounter more than once in his letters.

Any debate on the extent of the stylistic influence derived by Erasmus from modern languages inevitably raises the question of his acquaintance with other vernacular tongues besides his native Dutch. It has sometimes been supposed and even alleged, without reference to his works, that Erasmus knew nothing of these at all, or nothing for all practical purposes. This is unfounded, and the stories he tells (not only in his letters) would alone prove the falsity of the statement, even if there were no further evidence. It is true that when in Florence he was spoken to in Tuscan by Bernardo Ruccellai, he replied somewhat shortly 'surdo loqueris'. (Nor did he understand Canossa's Italian in Rome: *tandem dixit nescioquid Italice*.) But the case is very different with French. Here, apart from the many scenes described in the letters where Erasmus takes the lead in communication among travellers, for instance, or between travellers and townspeople, or even among townspeople themselves, as in the famous story in Allen 55, his testimony is sometimes quite explicit: e.g. (Allen 119): 'In Anglo nihil erat neque animi neque concilii neque linguae; nam Gallice prorsus nesciebat. Mihi . . .' etc. (ll. 149-150).

Erasmus quoted a French saying, *happe qui peust*, in the margin of the volume of Athenaeus that he used while editing the 1517 edition of the *Adages* (as Margaret Mann Phillips reports on p. 90 of her book *The Adages of Erasmus*). From the *De Recta Pronuntiatione* (*passim*, esp. 931 1ff.) it is quite clear that Erasmus knew vernacular idioms in French, Dutch and German. He understood, for example, and quotes as such, the argot of Parisian women: 'Idem faciunt hodie mulierculae Parisinae . . . sonantes . . . pro *ma mère, ma mèse.*'

The letters Erasmus wrote in England make it clear that he was not cut off from his fellow men in everyday affairs for want of the language; here, as with French, the tales he tells of himself show that he must have used as well as understood it (though his competence in French was certainly much greater). At the same time, he did not feel able to preach, or teach extensively, or write formal letters in English: 'Ut grex pastorem requireret, quem ego linguae ignarus praestare non poteram.' And he has to appeal to a friend to turn into English a rather difficult letter to the parent of a pupil. He spoke Latin at the tables of such men as Colet ('me aut mei similem adhibebat, quo Latinis fabulis declinaret profana colloquia'), and on the pilgrimage to St Thomas' shrine at Canterbury, the companion of Erasmus seems to have acted as interpreter; but there are indications that he acquired more than a working knowledge of the English language.

As for German, it is alluded to as if he knew it, and sometimes its expressions are borrowed, in his written works; and the letters show that he possessed a considerable command of the language. Dutch, of course, he always understood (e.g. Allen 9.2566 l. 219 and 2581 ll. 15–16. See also 5.1469 and 1.82 l.40.); and Dutch probably affected his Latin, at least in the frequent use of certain kinds of diminutive noun-forms. So much is claimed at least by Reedijk, the editor of Erasmus' poems; and he also points to the use of *fluitare* in the sense 'to be dripping wet', and suggests that here Erasmus is thinking of the Dutch verb *drijven* (C. Reedijk, *The Poems of Desiderius Erasmus*, Leyden 1956, p. 138n.). It must not be forgotten that, on Reedijk's dating, this poem was written in 1483 probably, when Erasmus was about fourteen years old and Dutch influence strongest.

Erasmus, it must be stressed (in spite of the extreme boldness of his use of unclassical language and especially of diminutives, where he much exceeds even the liberality in their use shown in his favourite patristic age as well as the practice of his own contemporaries), wrote a variety of Latin that was generally correct by classical standards. It seldom deviates from the rules of mood and tense, for example, in any way that ancient authors would not occasionally have permitted to themselves; and many if not most of the characteristics and peculiarities of his syntax have perfectly good classical antecedents. They are drawn, it must be said, from all the generations of Roman writers between Plautus and Macrobius; Erasmus is far from adopting the style and language of a single generation, let alone a single master such as Cicero. But none of it is incredible as Latin, or intolerable to a sensitive reader, like the Latin prose of Boccaccio, or the ambitious but decidedly awkward epistolary style of Coluccio Salutati; and it is all decidedly better in details than that of Petrarch—for example, he distinguishes accurately between *magis* and *plus* where Petrarch fails to do so. To find actual solecisms in the syntax and grammar of Erasmian Latin is singularly difficult. He has his deviations, and they are sometimes arresting enough; I have attempted to give a representative conspectus of these in another part of this chapter; but they amount to little more than stylistic signatures. We may prefer *video eum sedentem* to *video eum sedere*; but Plautus has the latter, and no doubt Erasmus is influenced by him. *Contentus* with an indicative, though his own, can easily be accounted for by a classical rule, even if not derived from a classical exemplar. If *utinam* is on occasion used with a primary tense of the subjunctive, this is quite common in the literature of the Republic: Plautus, Terence (especially) and even Cicero have it. And in his intermittent use of double compound tenses—of which I give a few examples elsewhere—he is surely thinking like a modern man (which need not, and I believe does not, imply that he is thinking in the idiom of a modern tongue): 'On sent que pour lui l'ancien participe passé a déjà perdu sa valeur temporelle.'[29]

While it would not be possible in a chapter such as this to attempt a comprehensive description, much less a grammar, of the language of Erasmus, the following *resumé* may help to illustrate some characteristics of Erasmian morphology and syntax. (Where names of editors are given, the bibliographical note at the end of the chapter should be consulted).

Nouns (cases): acc. after *sitire*; dat. after *proprius*; acc. of duration of time replaced by abl.; *post* with acc. replaced by *a* with abl.; *ad* with acc. replaced by dat. of purpose; abl. denoting quality, relation or instrument replaced by *in, ex* or *ab*; dat. of gerund after *par, aptus*, etc.; very frequent use of the acc. for gen., as in *id genus*; extended use of the gen., as in *bonitatis est hoc facere*; very frequent use of dat. of destination, as in *dare laudi*; dat. for *ad* with acc.; dat. of agent (or *per* with acc.) sometimes replacing *ab* with abl. of agent; noun as adj., e.g. *mundus hic praestigiator* (*Enchiridion Militis Christiani*, V. 1 A).

Adjectives; abl. *veteri*; many comparatives of the type *oculatior, picturatior, sitientior*, formally derived from participles; many superlatives formed from the perfect participle passive (e.g. *confusissimus*); variations on traditional formulae of indefinite number, e.g. *post dies aliquammultos*; expressions such as *te grandiusculus, post dies complusculos*; frequent use of adj. for adverb, as in *recens, demens*; adj. for noun, as in *grandaevi* 'old men', *simplices* 'the simple, simpletons'; also the idiom *quid multis?* instead of *quid multa?* There is an occasional preference for comparatives formed by the addition of *magis* over the inflected forms, in which it is tempting to see the influence of English (*cf. infra*, on prepositional *cum*).

Pronouns: pronominal *quid* (indef.) replaced by *quod*; prevalence, or at least fairly common occurence, of reflexive pronouns unrelated to the subject of the clause in which they occur (a tendency shared with other Humanists, Thomas More for example;[30] *tantus labor* preferred to *tot labores*; *honestas*, for example, often replaced by *quod honestum est*, possibly under the influence of

Greek; *unusquisque*, with *suus*, for *quisque*; *si quisquam* for *si quis*; and *quisque=quicumque* (archaic).

Adverbs: *gratanter* (in verse); *adhuc=nunc*; *huc=ad hoc* (purpose); *magis=magis magisque*; *quam* for *quantum*, with verb; *an* or *annon* for *num*, *-ne* or *nonne* (e.g. *annon absurde?* in a parenthesis); *aeque* for *tam* with adverb; *hic* 'in this case'; *tantum=tam* with adj.; *quando=cum* (with *tum*); *nimis quam=perquam*; *tantum non=μονὸν οὐ* (perhaps a Grecism of Erasmus' own, though it occurs once in Livy); *ut=*'how' (exclamatory, e.g. *ut violentus es!*); *in tantum* in the sense 'to such a degree'; *utcumque* in that of 'altogether' or 'as a whole'; *longe* (with *plus*) replacing *multum*; *tamen* (after a concessive) left to be understood; *tantum–quantum* replacing *tot–quot*; *tanto* replacing *tam multo*; *ex adverso* for *adversus*, as in certain passages of Livy and Pliny. *Dumtaxat*[31] and *subinde*[32] are made to work exceedingly hard; and Erasmus derived from Cicero a proclivity for adverbs ending in *-im*.

Prepositions: *absque* is often used for *sine* (Aulus Gellius may be the source of this, but it occurs also in Plautus and Terence); *in*, expressing result (Sallust, Virgil, Tacitus) and also replacing *ad*; *gratia* replacing *ob*; *post* 'because of'; *ad* replacing *contra*; *pro* 'in favour of'; *cum* in several hardly classical senses, which for the most part, as Remy and Dunil-Marquebreucq suggest, seem to reflect the influence of English or Dutch usage; phrases like *conducibilis ad*; *in summa* for *ad summa*; and *praeter* loosely used to replace a clause with *nisi* etc., e.g. 884 A *fatuus nihil differt ab animante bruto praeter formam corporis*.

Conjunctions: *siquidem* is regularly used for 'since', in the manner of Latin authors of the later Roman period; *alius quam* for *alius ac*; *quo* (without comparative) for final *ut*, e.g. *quo sint obvia*; *ubi* for *cum* 'whenever'; *quod aiunt* for *ut aiunt*; *quod* with subjunctive for *ut* consecutive; *quod* with subjunctive in statements with causal overtones, e.g. *admiror–quod mutarint*; *nec* for *ne quidem*; *sed* as a variation of *et*, in the manner of Sallust (e.g. *sed eadem fugacissima*); *simul et* instead of *et*; *sed esto* or *verum esto* (with subjunctive) 'granting that . . .'; *posteaquam* (with subjunctive) for *postquam* 'since'; *ceu* 'as, like' (Virgil and Silver Latinity); *modo ut/ne* or *tantum ut*, for *dummodo* (also *dum ut*, as an adaptation by analogy of *dum ne*); *nisi si* 'except if'; *perinde quasi* as a kind of fusion of *perinde ac si* and *proinde quasi*; *quin* and *quamquam* often='all the same'; *et* sometimes substituted for *sed*; *idem et* for *idem ac*; *simul et* for *simul ac*; also *iuxta ac* (*Querela Pacis*, preface); frequent use of *ut ne* (e.g. *ut ne quid addam*); sometimes a relative replacing *dummodo*, e.g. *quae vacent* replacing *dummodo vacent* (521 D).

Mood of verbs: After *cum*, Erasmus sometimes moves from indicative to subjunctive; frequently he puts *erat* for *esset*, *poterat* for *potuisset*, which has good classical antecedents; e.g. *praestiterat vivum sepeliri* and *dissilierat, nisi cessisset*; like Terence, he has *tametsi* with subjunctive; with *utinam* he uses either primary or secondary tenses of the subj.; Margolin finds in him a somewhat extended use of modal attraction, but, as his editors generally acknowledge, in the uses of moods (a matter in which deviation is frequent even among ancient authors), Erasmus is on the whole classical. Occasionally we find pres. or perf. subj. after *quisquis*; explanatory clauses, which regularly require the subj., are found in the indic. mood; and indefinite *qui* is similarly found with the indicative. It is possible to find subj. for indic. of the 'true' reason, as in *non quod metuerem . . . sed quod sis . . . .*

Tense: Like other Humanists (Petrarch is an obvious example, and an author as careful as More is another), Erasmus takes the rule or principle of sequence of tenses lightly on occasion; this is more noticeable in those works the style of which is conversational, and where a deliberate search for 'flexibility' would not be out of place, namely the *Letters* and the *Colloquies*. In fact, Erasmus' liberties are hardly different in degree from those taken by the best authors, including Cicero in his letters, and here again he is remarkably classical. He is prone like other Humanists, again, to indulge from time to time in double compound tenses (e.g. *delapsus fuerat, exstinctus fui, passus fuisset, si confessus fuisset*). The future participle *nasciturus* is taken, with so much else in Erasmian Latinity, from the Vulgate (*Judges* 13.8).

Voice: The passive is notably favoured, and sometimes over-done, as when we find e.g. *ventum est a quibusdam* (for *quidam venerunt*), and *discebantur a christianis* (for *christiani discebant*). In such cases it is to be suspected that the 'agent' was added as clarification by an after-thought; one more effect and proof of the fact that Erasmus habitually wrote *praecipitanter* and rarely retraced his steps to blot or to change a word. One can see this in a typical phrase like *concursum est a pluribus*. There is much use of the impersonal third person singular of the passive, which (as Margolin remarks) gives a sententious tone: e.g. *immodico studio paratur possessio*; also *dici vix potest quantum* . . . and *in eo praedicatur dexteritas.* We also find *indultum est* (*De sarcienda ecclesiae concordia* 13) and *impertiri deponent* (*Praise of Folly* 140). The boldness of the last example amply illustrates the Erasmian love of passive constructions. *Cf.* Crahay-Delcourt *Douze lettres* p. 67: Loca tum festinanti praeterita adicio, 'I am adding passages which I previously omitted in haste.'

Constructions with verbs: *ut* with the subjunctive in place of the infinitive after, for example, *decorum est*; omission of *ut* as in *fac evolvas*, or *facit salutetur* (774 F); use of the poetic idiom *sum facilis dare*; much use of the subordinate clause introduced by *quod*, 'the fact that'; *ut* with subjunctive after *iubere*, and *ne* with the subjunctive after *vetare* (perhaps by analogy); infinitive after *videre* when the sense would appear to demand a participle; a peculiar use of *contentus* with the indicative in a quasi-adverbial sense; two abl. abs. linked by a relative (*his neglectis quibus subductis* . . .); a pronounced addiction to *ad* with the gerund, e.g. *ad vera dicendum appositissimus* (*Hieronymi Stridon. vita* 45),[33] *ad feliciter emigrandum pertinere* (810 F); use of the passive voice and infinitive in phrases like *deprehendebantur Augustini non esse*, 'It was detected that they were not written by Augustine' (*Augustini Opera, tom.* ii, edition of 1528, preface *sub init.*; not included in *Opera Omnia* or Allen); extremely frequent use of *curare* with gerund or gerundive; *esse* with dat. of gerund, e.g. *esse oneri ferendo*; love of the form *ausim*, e.g. *illud ausim affirmare, non ausim iudicare*, etc.; the use of the present participle with adjectival significance in association with a genitive, e.g. *lucri appetens*, or with *ad* plus accusative, e.g. *subfrivola quaestio nec multum faciens ad pietatem*; typical also of Erasmus' rather hurried style are expressions like *tanta cautio fuit ne* . . . Often there is a verb suppressed in association with a future participle, as in e.g. *dicam, sed vereor ne imitatur* (864 E.). The verb *spero* is quite often used parenthetically, like *credo*, e.g. in snatches of dialogue like this: '*Christus dignetur* . . . *Spero dignabitur.*'

NOTES

Bibliographical Note: No study devoted solely to Erasmian Latinity appears, at the date of writing, to have been published in any language. Discussions of the style, grammar (or syntax) and vocabulary of Erasmus, as these are exhibited in particular works or groups of letters, are to be found in: R.

Crahay and M. Delcourt (eds.), *Douze lettres d'Erasme*, Paris, 1938; Y. Remy and R. Dunil-Marquebreucq (eds. and trs.), *Erasme: Dulce bellum inexpertis*, Collection Latomus, VIII, Brussels, 1953; and J.-C. Margolin (ed.), *Erasme: Declamatio de Pueris statim ac liberaliter Educandis*, Travaux d'Humanisme et Renaissance, LXXVII, Geneva, 1966. To all of these I am indebted.

Opera Omnia refers to *Desiderii Erasmi Roterodami Opera Omnia*, ed. J. Clericus (10t. in 11 vols), Leyden, 1703–1706.

I should like to thank Professor F. D. Hoeniger and the Reverend G. A. D. Scott for kind assistance given to me in using the collection of Erasmian and other material at the Centre for Reformation and Renaissance Studies in the library of Victoria College, Toronto.

[1] *Ciceronianus* (*Opera Omnia*, I. 1008 E): 'vix est in manibus'. Erasmus criticizes Petrarch's style both here and in the *Letters* (Allen, XI. 208).

[2] 'So schreibt auch Erasmus aus der Notwendigkeit der jeweiligen Situation heraus, rasch, ohne grosse Vorarbeiten, in diesem Sinn journalistisch.' (W. Rüegg, *Cicero und der Humanismus*, Zürich, 1946, p. 85).

[3] A typical example of Erasmian ellipse is 'O miram inconstantiam, qui . . .' (Crahay-Delcourt, *Douze Lettres*, p. 69). Erasmus habitually writes *pro mea virili* or simply *pro virili* (omitting *parte*). For examples of anacoluthon and similar devices, see Margolin p. 609.

[4] H. W. Garrod, *The Study of Good Letters* (Oxford University Press, 1963), p. 95.

[5] In Allen, III. 473ff. (914), Longolius characterizes the Latin of Budé ('nervi, spiritus, sanguis') and of Erasmus ('plus carnis, cutis, coloris'); Erasmus is 'creber facetiis'. In Allen, III. 521 (935), Erasmus writes to Longolius about the style of Budé; see also II. 567.

[6] 'Nulla est ars humana, cui non concedimus ius utendi suis vocabulis' remarks Erasmus (*Opera Omnia*, I. 996 E). There are however observations on the dangers of jargon in the *De Recta Pronuntiatione* (*Opera Omnia*, I, 930).

[7] It is fair to say that in Erasmus' Colloquy' Ἰχθυοφαγία the phrase *miraculorum architectrix* may be found—once.

[8] Coinages by More have a family likeness to those attributed to Erasmus: see the list of words, said to be of More's invention, given in Delcourt's edition of the *Utopia* and quoted in the Yale edition of More's works, IV. 582. One or two of these are in fact to be found in Erasmus, but this in itself does not disprove More's paternity.

[9] Crahay-Delcourt, *Douze Lettres*, p. 20.

[10] Allen, IV. 523 (1211).

[11] Yet it must be remembered that Erasmus was distinguished from early years by a brilliant grasp of classical metre, both in theory and (as the *Convivium Poeticum* alone would amply demonstrate) in practice; cf. also The colloquy *Impostura*.

[12] On the variety of epistolary styles, see Erasmus' discussion in the introduction to the *De Ratione Conscribendi Epistolas* (*Opera Omnia*, I. 345 A) and ch. III. of this volume.

[13] Allen, XI. 207 (3043).

[14] Allen, I. 69 (IV).

[15] *Ciceronianus* (*Opera Omnia*, I. 1013 E). The whole passage should be noted, making allowance for self-caricature.

[16] P. S. Allen, *Erasmus: Lectures and Wayfaring Sketches*, Oxford University Press, 1934, pp. 17–20, 56.

[17] *Vide supra* p. 118 and note 10.

[18] If indeed they are Pattison's. The joint article signed by Pattison and P. S. Allen which appeared in *Encyclopaedia Britannica* (11th ed.), IX. 731–2 contains perhaps the most judicious and best informed brief statement in English on the subject of Erasmus' style. I have never seen the proof of the usual attribution of this part of the article to Pattison.

[19] *De Conscribendis Epistolis, Omnia Opera*, I. 347 D.

[20] It is not generally realized that Erasmus made a serious study of Cicero's *clausulae*: see *Opera Omnia*, I. 975 C and 1007 E.

[21] First published in 1535.

[22] The expression is Eduard Norden's (*Antike Kunstprosa*, Leipzig, 1909, II. 778 n. 1).

[23] On the delicate question of the relative frequency of various classes of diminutives in different kinds of diction in late Latin see Frederic T. Cooper, *Word Formation in the Roman Sermo Plebeius*, New York, 1895, especially ch. III.

[24] *Ciceronianus, Opera Omnia*, I. 976 C.

[25] Text as edited by A. Hyma in *The Youth of Erasmus*, Ann Arbor, Michigan, 1930, p. 263.

[26] *V.* J.-C. Margolin (ed.), *Declamatio de pueris*, p. 601.

[27] E.g. *agonotheta, amphibologia, bulimia, catapotia, cephalalgia, chalcographus, chirotheca, daduchi, digamia, gastromargia, genethliaci* ('casters of nativities'), *grammatophorus, heptatechnus, holocautoma, monotechnus, ogdoas, orniropoli, ptochotyranni, polyphagia, polyposia, poppysmus, soloecus, thymiama*. For Greek words in Erasmus' poetry, *v.* Margolin, p. 23 and Reedijk, *Poems of Desiderius Erasmus*, Leyden, 1956, p. 114. I do not include technical terms of grammar or rhetoric, and have tried to exclude ecclesiastical terms.

[28] Vide Supra p. 117.

[29] Crahay-Delcourt, p. 24; echoed by Margolin, p. 616.

[30] The Yale edition of the Complete Works of Sir Thomas More, vol. IV (Utopia), ed. Edward Surtz, S. J., and J. H. Hexter: Yale University Press, 1965.

[31] In the *Spongia* (against Hutten), Erasmus writes, 'Non arbitror quemquam pontificem, duntaxat hunc. . . .' The editor of Hutten's works, E. Höcking, took violent exception to this use of *duntaxat*, and wrote a footnote beginning thus: 'Latine dicendum erat aut *praeter hunc*, si ironice, aut *nedum sive certe non hunc*, si simpliciter negandum erat. . . .' *Hutteni Opera*, Leipzig, 1859–61, rep. Aalen, 1963, II, 301.

[32] In the *Ciceronianus, Opera Omnia*, I. 986 E, Erasmus noted that the Ciceronians would write *identidem* for his *subinde*.

[33] W. K. Ferguson, *Erasmi Opuscula*, The Hague, 1933, p. 135.

VI

The Middle Ages, Erasmus and the Modern Reader

T. A. DOREY

ERASMUS came near the end of almost two thousand years of Latin literature. Stretching back into the third century in verse, with Naevius and Livius Andronicus as its earliest representatives, and in prose to the middle of the second century B.C., when Cato the Censor first made Latin a suitable vehicle for literary expression, it reached its highest level in the two hundred years between the dictatorship of Sulla, when Cicero made his first important speech, and the reign of Hadrian, which saw the deaths of Suetonius and Juvenal. But even after the close of the Silver Age there were great writers, though their appearance was sporadic: Fronto, in the second century, Ammianus Marcellinus, Ausonius and Claudian in the fourth, and, at the beginning of the fifth century, the great Christian writers St Augustine and St Jerome, who as literary figures can be classed with the most important men of the purely Classical age.

Even during the Dark Ages the writing of Latin of a high standard did not quite die out; on the continent the *Gesta Francorum* of Gregory of Tours and in England Bede's *Ecclesiastical History* were works of considerable merit. But it was after the reign of Charlemagne that Latin literature took on a new life. A leading member of the Emperor's court, Einhard of Fulda, wrote a biography of Charlemagne that was modelled on Suetonius' *Lives of the Caesars*. This was the first secular biography of the Middle Ages, and it had very great influence. It affected Asser's *Life of Alfred*, in which the Suetonian elements are probably derived from Einhard and not directly from Suetonius, while two hundred years later phrases used by Einhard in describing the physical appearance and personal habits of Charlemagne were inserted by an unknown interpolator into William of Jumièges' account of another great monarch, William the Conqueror. Apart from the influence of Suetonius on biographical and historical writing in the centuries after Charlemagne, with its interest in the physical appearance of the subject and the technique of portraying a man's character by giving examples of his various individual qualities, the Carolingian age saw the birth of an interest in secular Latin literature for its own sake and a widespread search for manuscripts of Classical authors.

The exploits of William the Conqueror inspired a number of laudatory biographies, notably the *Gesta Normannorum Ducum* of William of Jumièges, tracing the history of the Dukes of Normandy, and the *Gesta Guillelmi Ducis* of William of Poitiers, in which the Conqueror is portrayed as a paragon of all virtues, a second and greater Caesar, a new—and no less pious—Aeneas. This latter work is full of propaganda, but it shows a wide knowledge of Classical history and mythology and acquaintance with numerous Latin authors, including Caesar, Virgil, Suetonius, Cicero, Sallust, Statius and Juvenal. But it was in the twelfth century that this Renaissance of Latin literature, as it may well be called, came to its full flower, in a great humanistic revival to which the University of Paris made a most important contribution. The great figures of this period were men of considerable intellectual capacity who had a profound knowledge of such Classical Latin authors as were then available. To mention only those writers who flourished in England, the most important were William of Malmesbury at the beginning of the century, Aelred of Rievaulx, John of Salisbury, who had been a pupil of Abelard and became Becket's secretary, and, at the end of the century, the stormy petrel of Welsh ecclesiastical politics, Giraldus Cambrensis. At the lower level, though not inferior in purely literary skill, were Eadmer, the friend and biographer of Anselm, Henry of Huntingdon, whose *Historia Anglorum* is eminently readable but contains a large amount of what a character in Gilbert and Sullivan's 'Mikado' described as 'merely corroborative detail, to lend an air of verisimilitude to an otherwise bald and unconvincing narrative', Robert, Bishop of Bath, whose *Gesta Stephani* gives a vigorous and reasonably impartial account of the Civil War, and Geoffrey of Monmouth, who wrote the famous *Historia Britonum* with its romantic expansion of the Arthurian legend.

After the twelfth century a period of decline set in, and though there were many competent performers—amongst them William of Newbury and Matthew Paris—Latin literature did not reach such great heights again until the time of Erasmus. It will perhaps be worthwhile to make a comparison as regards certain literary aspects of their work between Erasmus himself and some of the more important writers of this period.

William of Jumièges wrote in a plain, pedestrian style, with occasional ornamentation by some unusual poetic word. He made frequent use of participles, especially the ablative absolute, and connecting relatives: these were his two main literary devices. His narrative style was simple and straightforward, usually consisting of a number of short clauses loosely connected together. The following passage, describing William's landing in England, is typical:

> Inde vero, vento flante secundo, velis in sublime pansis, trans mare Penevesellum appulit, ubi statim firmissimo vallo castrum condidit. Quod militibus committens, festinus Hastingas venit, ibique cito opere aliud firmavit. Quem Heraldus incautum accelerans praeoccupare, contracta Anglorum innumera multitudine, tota nocte equitans in campo belli mane apparuit. (VII. 14)

> Then, with a fair wind blowing, he spread his sails aloft and crossed the sea to Pevensey, where at once he built a fort with a strong rampart. Entrusting this to his knights he came without delay to Hastings, and here he quickly built another fort. Harold, hurrying in order to catch him off his guard, having gathered together a vast horde of English, rode all through the night and appeared in the morning on the field of battle.

As an example of the slightly more elevated style used at a dramatic climax:

> Quo triumpho inter tanta pericula eo ordine confecto dux noster inclitarum virtutum, et quem nostri praeconia stili minime sufficiunt aequare, in die Natalis Domini, ab omnibus tam Normannorum quam Anglorum proceribus rex electus, sacro oleo ab episcopis regni delibutus, ac regali diademate coronatus, sub millesimo sexagesimo sexto ab incarnatione Domini anno. (VII. 16.)

> When this glorious victory had been finally won in this way amidst such great dangers, our duke, a man of outstanding merit, whom the praises of my pen can never properly match, on Christmas Day was chosen king by all the nobles both Norman and English, annointed with the holy oil by the bishops of the

realm, and crowned with the royal diadem, in the one thousand and sixty-sixth year from the Incarnation of Our Lord.

Eadmer wrote the *Historia Novorum*, dealing with English ecclesiastical history between 1066 and 1122, in a lucid style that aroused the admiration of his younger contemporary, William of Malmesbury. He had great powers of vivid description, particularly in the representation of conversations, in which he would give the actual words of the speaker as if he himself had been an eyewitness. His account of the investiture of Anselm as Archbishop against his will is highly dramatic:

> At illi animati in eum, seque ipsos pro mora quam objectionibus ipsius intendendo passi sunt ignaviae redarguentes, 'Virgam huc pastoralem, virgam' clamitant 'pastoralem'. Et arrepto brachio eius dextro, alii renitentem trahere, alii impellere, lectoque iacentis coeperunt applicare. Rege autem ei baculum porrigente, manum contra clausit, et eum suscipere nequaquam consensit. Episcopi vero digitos eius strictim volae infixos erigere conati sunt, quo vel sic manui eius baculus ingereretur. Verum cum in hoc conatum suum aliquandiu frustra expenderent, et ipse pro sua quam patiebatur laesione verba dolentis ederet, tandem, indice levato sed protinus ab eo reflexo, clausae manui eius baculus appositus est, et episcoporum manibus cum eadem manu compressus atque retentus. Acclamante autem multitudine 'Vivat episcopus, vivat', episcopi cum clero sublimi voce hymnum 'Te Deum laudamus' decantare coepere, electumque pontificem portaverunt potius quam deuxerunt in vicinam ecclesiam, ipso modis quibus poterat resistente atque dicente 'Nihil est quod facitis; nihil est quod facitis'. (*Historia Novorum* I. 41.)

But they became angry with him and accused themselves of cowardice for the delay they had incurred by listening to his objections, and began to shout, 'Bring here the pastoral staff, bring the pastoral staff'. Then they seized his right arm, and in spite of his struggles, with some pulling and some pushing, they began to force him towards the sick-bed. The king held out the staff, but he clenched his fist against it and absolutely refused to take it. Then the bishops tried to force up his fingers that he had dug tightly into his palm, so as to thrust the staff into his hand like that. But when they had wasted their efforts for some time at this and he was uttering words of pain over the hurt that he was suffering, and when at last they had pushed back his forefinger but he had at once bent it down again, they placed the staff against his clenched fist and the bishops pressed it and held it with their hands against his hand. Then the crowd cried out, 'Long live the archbishop, long live the archbishop', and the bishops and clergy began to chant the 'Te

Deum' in a loud voice, and they carried rather than led their chosen prelate into a neighbouring church, with Anselm resisting in whatever way he could and repeating, 'What you do is null and void, what you do is null and void.'

However, in some parts of Eadmer's works the sentences are longer and more involved, and the thought, especially in connection with theological ideas, is expressed with less clarity.

William of Malmesbury was a most prolific writer, compiling books on theology, ecclesiastical ritual and law as well as his histories and biographies, but his most important works were the *Gesta Regum*, a deliberate continuation of Bede, and the unfinished *Historia Novella*, a contemporary account of the Civil War. His style was elegant, though sometimes compressed. He made good use of imagery, as in his description of the early death of the Conqueror's son Richard:

> Sed tantam primaevi floris indolem mors acerba cito depasta corrupit (*Gesta Regum* III. 275).

> But untimely death all too soon fed upon the genius of his unripe bloom and spoiled it.

He could also employ a shrewd epigram to great effect, as he did on the death of Roger, Bishop of Salisbury:

> Extremum puto calamitatis, cuius etiam me miseret, quod, cum multis miser videretur, paucissimis erat miserabilis. (*Historia Novella* II. 32.)

> The most disastrous thing that befell him, for which even I feel sorry, was that though many people regarded him as pitiable, very few showed him any pity.

William had read widely, and quoted extensively from Classical Latin authors, but his method in using them is not always above criticism. For example, he purports to quote Livy in describing Robert of Gloucester's arrival in England (*Historia Novella* II. 29) when in fact he is quoting Orosius, and much of his discussion on the difference between true and false liberality (*Gesta Regum* IV. 313) is taken almost verbatim and without acknowledgment from Cicero, *De Officiis* II. 56. He enlivened his history with anecdotes, which he told with great skill, whether it be the miraculous stories that his readers expected from their historians, like the tale of the dancers in the church-yard or the witch of Berkley, or the more mundane story of William Rufus and his boots:

Cum calciaretur novas caligas, interrogavit cubicularium quanti constitissent: cum ille respondit tres solidos, indignabundus et fremens ait: 'Ex quo habet rex caligas tam exilis pretii? vade et affer mihi emptas marci argenti.' Ivit ille, et multo viliores afferens, quanti praeceperat emptas ementitus est. 'Atqui' inquit rex, 'Istae regiae conveniunt maiestati.' (*Gesta Regum* IV. 313.)

When he was putting on some new boots, he asked the chamberlain how much they had cost. When the man answered, 'Three shillings,' William lost his temper, gnashed his teeth and said, 'Since when has a king had boots of such a paltry price? Go and get me a pair that cost a silver mark.' The chamberlain went off, got some much cheaper boots, and falsely said that they had cost what the king had ordered him to pay. 'There,' said the king, 'these are boots that suit a royal majesty.'

The *Gesta Stephani*, of which Robert, Bishop of Bath was probably the author, gives a contemporary account of the Civil War written by a supporter of Stephen. It was composed after the war, and contains no dates. The style is forceful, and at times slightly rhetorical with bursts of moral indignation. The sentences are rather long and complex, often composed of a number of participal clauses, but the narrative is fast-moving and at times dramatic. A good example is the surprise attack on Matilda's camp made by the desperate Londoners:

Cum ergo comitissa quid super postulatione sua cives responderent, voluntatis implendae secura, praestolaretur, omnis civitas sonantibus ubique campanis, signum videlicet ad bellum progrediendi, ad arma convolavit, omnesque unum habentes animum in comitissam et suos atrocissime irruere velle, quasi frequentissima ex apium alveariis examina reseratis portis pariter prodierunt. Illa autem cum coquinatis dapibus nimium audacter nimiumque secure recumbere iam proposuisset, audito civitatis horrendo tumultu, et a quodam de proditione in eam concitata secrete permonita, fugae velocissime praesidium cum omnibus suis expetiit. Cumque cursatiles ascensi equos vix antemurales civitatis domos fugiendo liquissent, ecce civium magna dictuque et aestimatu indicibilis copia hospitia quae reliquerant subiens, quodcumque impraemeditata fugae velocitas intus deseruerat, sicut relictum invenit, ita et inventum ubique diripuit. (*Gesta Stephani* I. 62.)

So when the countess was waiting to see what the citizens would reply to her demand, confident that she would get her way, the whole city, with bells ringing everywhere as a signal to go to war, rushed to arms, and all with one single feeling, the desire to fling themselves savagely upon the countess and her followers, like a swarm of bees coming out of a hive, flung open the gates and issued forth in a body. Matilda, all too boldly and all too heedlessly, was now intending to take her seat at the banquet that had been cooked, but hearing the horrifying uproar from the city and having been warned secretly by some individual of the treason that had been fomented against her, she and all her companions lost no time in seeking safety by flight. Mounted on fast horses they had barely got clear of the suburbs when behold! A horde of townsfolk, too large for words or reckoning, entered the abandoned lodgings, and whatever the hasty and unpremeditated flight had left behind within, they found just as it was left, and just as they found it they pillaged it.

From a purely literary point of view one of the most interesting writers of this period is Henry of Huntingdon, in whose hands, as can also be said of Geoffrey of Monmouth, the writing of history did not aim at the establishment of a truthful record of events but at the production of an elegant and artistic piece of prose. Henry took exceptional care in the construction of his sentences. Many of them were composed of a series of balanced clauses, often deliberately grouped together in pairs, in fours, but most of all in threes, and considerable use was made of rhyme. There is a good example of his technique at the start of his prologue. The opening words are: 'Cum in omni fere literarum studio dulce laboris lenimen et summum doloris solamen, dum vivitur, insitum considerem,' where there is a careful balance between the two phrases beginning with *dulce* and *summum* and a deliberate rhyming of *doloris solamen* with *laboris lenimen*. Then he goes on to commend history as being more effective than philosophy for teaching the difference between virtue and vice, taking as his example the history of Homer:

> Homerus autem . . . prudentiam Ulysis, fortitudinem Agamemnonis, temperantiam Nestoris, iustitiam Menelai; et e contra imprudentiam Aiacis, debilitatem Priami, intemperantiam Achillis, iniustitiam Paridis, honestum et utile, et his contraria, lucidius et delectabilius philosophis historiando disseruit.

> But Homer, in writing history, discoursed in a manner more lucid and more enjoyable than did the philosophers about the wisdom of Ulysses, the valour of Agamemnon, the temperance of Nestor, and the justice of Menelaus; and on the contrary, about the folly of Ajax, the feebleness of Priam, the intemperance of Achilles, and the injustice of Paris, qualities good and profitable and their opposites.

Here there is a group of four qualities opposed by an antithetic group of four contrasting qualities. This is a device that Henry often uses. In his account of the Siege of Nicaea in the First Crusade there is a list of nouns that fall naturally into a series of opposing pairs:

> Paganis non sagittae, non tela, non ligna, non lapides, non fragmenta, non moles, non aqua, non ignis, non ars, non vires, non prosunt missilia amentata (*Historia Anglorum* VII. 6).

> Neither arrows nor darts, neither sticks nor stones, neither chips of rocks nor chunks of masonry, neither water nor fire, neither skill nor strength, nor volleys of missiles were of any help to the heathen.

There are frequent examples of his use of rhyme in the fictitious speeches that, following the example of Classical historians, he includes in his work. In the Earl of Gloucester's speech before the battle of Lincoln, there are several instances: Ad agendum volubilis, ad relinquendum immobilis. . . . Baccho devotus, Marti ignotus, vino redolens, bellis insolens . . . latrociniis assueti, rapinis delibuti, homicidiis saginati, omnes tandem periuria contaminati . . . ille instruxit, iste destruxit. (VIII. 15.) He is also fond of alliteration and assonance: pondus proelii diu pertulisset (IV. 11); semina sua seminaverunt, ut venientes veniant (IV. 16).

Henry's battle-scenes were set out in an epic idiom that would have done credit to his hero, Homer. The details are usually conventional. There is *stridor* and *clamor*; the noise is flung back by surrounding hills or town-walls; *resonuerunt montes et colles* (VIII. 9), *resonabant colles, resonabant muralia urbis* (VIII. 18); sparks fly out from the clash of steel on steel: *horribiles tinnitus et igneas collisiones* (VI. 13); *ignitas collisiones, formidabiles tinnitus* (V. 16); *ignem prosilientem ex galearum et gladiorum collisione* (VIII. 18).

He loves the sensational, and when he records supernatural occurrences, such as blood bubbling up from the ground or from walls, or God's vengeance falling upon the wicked, he does so not for the edification of his readers or in a spirit of moral indignation, but purely for its literary effect. His whole work is notable for his very careful choice and arrangement of words with particular attention to their sound; even though the final result appears at times deliberately contrived and banal, at its best his style can rise to great heights. For example, in spite of the conventional presentation, his description of the capture of Stephen at Lincoln is a most vivid piece of writing:

Tum apparuit vis regis fulminea, bipenni maxima caedens hos, diruens illos. Tunc novus oritur clamor; omnes in eum, ipse in omnes. Tandem regia bipennis ex ictuum frequentia confracta est. Ipse gladio abstracto dextra regis digno, rem mirabiliter agit, donec et gladius confractus est. Quod videns Guillelmus de Kahaines, miles validissimus, irruit in regem, et eum galea arripiens voce magna clamavit: 'Huc omnes, huc! regem teneo.' Advolant omnes et capitur rex. (VIII. 18.)

Then was displayed the king's strength, like a thunderbolt, as with a mighty axe he cut down some and scattered others. Then arose a fresh uproar; all were against him, and he against all. At last the king's axe was shattered from its many blows. He drew a sword worthy of a king's right hand and fought like a hero until the sword too, was shattered. Seeing this, William of Kahaines, a stalwart knight, rushed on the king, and seizing him by the helmet cried out in a loud voice: 'Come here, all of you, come here. I have the king.' They all rushed up, and the king was captured.

Aelred of Rievaulx followed and improved on Henry's style, using his technique in a more subtle and sophisticated manner. There was the same careful choice and arrangement of words, but greater variation and new stylistic devices. There is the same emphasis on noise in battle-descriptions:

Sequitur lituum stridor, tubarum crepitus, fragor lancearum percutientium alteram ad alteram; tremit terra, fremit caelum, echo vicini montes collesque resultant. (*Relatio de Standardo* f. 200.)

There follows the blare of horns, the blast of trumpets, the clash of lances striking upon each other; the earth trembles, the sky roars, and the nearby mountains and hills fling back the echo.

Similarly:

Circa galeata capita gladii tinniunt, collisione metallorum scintillae prorumpunt (*De genealogia regum: de rege Edmundo*).

About their helmeted heads their swords ring; from the clash of steel on steel sparks shoot forth.

There is the same love of assonance, rhyme and balance of words. In his description of King David of Scotland:

Quem mansuetudo amabilem, iustitia terribilem, castitas compositum, humilitas communem fecerat (*De genealogia: de sancto rege Scottorum David*).

Whose mercifulness made him loved, whose justice made him feared, whose chastity made him sober, and whose humility made him free from pride.

Such noble qualities were important in a king,

> Cuius vitiis facile favent inferiores, proni ad imitandum, prompti ad adulandum, cum et impunitas praestet audaciam, libido vero acuat et accendat luxuriam (*De genealogia, loc. cit.*).

> Whose vices are readily condoned by subjects quick to imitate and eager to flatter, since freedom from punishment gives them boldness and lust sharpens and fires their wantonness!

At times the clauses are varied by the use of chiasmus: 'Et ampliavit possessionibus et honoribus cumulavit' (*De genealogia, loc. cit.*) and, 'singulis verbis ipse intenderet, ipse singulis orationibus responderet' (*De genealogia, loc. cit.*).

In Aelred's works, particularly in the *Relatio de Standardo*, there are echoes of Virgil and Cicero that show the deepening influence of the Classical authors during the course of the twelfth century. John of Salisbury, the most important figure of the next generation, deliberately modelled his style on Cicero, and brought Latin style one stage nearer to the artificial Ciceronianism that was in vogue in the lifetime of Erasmus. John of Salisbury's most important work was the *Polycraticus*, in which he outlined the ideal state in a fusion of Platonic and Christian terms, in which the Prince represented the head of the political organism, but the clergy represented the soul. The doctrine put forward in this work, that the temporal power was subordinate to the church, was significant in relation to the struggle between Henry II and Becket.

Giraldus Cambrensis, at the turn of the century, marked the decline of the era. He was a voluminous writer, and his works included an autobiography, in which he records his efforts to set aside the annulment of his election as Bishop of St David's, an account of a journey through Wales preaching the Crusade with Archbishop Baldwin, a description of that country and its inhabitants, an account of Prince John's expedition to Ireland, with a description of the country, and numerous other compositions. He had a keen wit and sense of humour, great powers of observation, and immense skill as a raconteur, but his style was overelaborate and affected, and he was too fond of making a parade of his learning.

Compared with even the finest Latin writers of the twelfth century, Erasmus' style shows a naturalness, lightness, and elegance that was partly due to his own genius, partly to the fact that, to him more than any of them, Latin was the equivalent of his mother tongue, and partly to the vastly enriched knowledge of the best Classical authors, both Latin and Greek, that had come into being during the course of the Renaissance. The writers of the twelfth century generally knew little or no Greek. Their range of Latin authors was limited: Cicero's philosophical and rhetorical works, particularly the *De Oratore* and the *De Officiis*, Sallust, Horace, Virgil, Caesar, Statius, Lucan, Juvenal and Suetonius, together with late writers such as Florus, Orosius, Martianus Capella, and the Christian Fathers, formed the staple literary diet, and the idioms and vocabulary of these authors were used indiscriminately.

Cicero's speeches were little known, and his letters not at all. Livy was seldom read, and the most popular models for historical composition were Sallust and Suetonius. The standards for syntax and grammatical usage were derived, not from the rules established in Classical times, but from those of the Carolingian age, when Charlemagne's educational reforms, carried out under the direction of Alcuin of York, succeeded in preventing a breakdown of communication between literate men in western Europe by fixing certain norms not only for handwriting—the celebrated Carolingian minuscule—but also for the Latin language itself. Up till then the forms of Latin spoken and written in different parts of Europe had become so varied according to different local usages that Latin was well on the way to breaking up into the several Romance languages that succeeded it. The reforms of Charlemagne called a halt to this process, as far as the language of court, literature, and officialdom was concerned. But the clock could not be put back completely, and the many elements of low Latin, colloquial Latin, or church Latin, and the many foreign words or altered meanings to Classical words, still remained.

There was still the blurring of the precise distinction between cases, tenses and moods. Sometimes the subjunctive might be used in a subordinate clause, sometimes the indicative. The various past tenses were employed without much discrimination. Indirect statement might be expressed by the accusative and infinitive construction, or by some conjunction such as *quod*, *quia*, or *quoniam* with either the subjunctive or the indicative. Often *quod* was used instead of *ut* to introduce a clause expressing result. The comparative of adjectives and adverbs was often employed as the equivalent of either the positive or the superlative. *Unus* was frequently used as an indefinite article, *ille* as a definite article. The pronouns *ipse* and *idem* were used as a synonym of *is*. There was a tendency to use the infinitive loosely to express purpose or obligation, especially after *facio* and *habeo*.

These and other similar pecularities—one might well call them solecisms—of medieval Latin found little place in the Latin of Erasmus, who returned to grammatical and syntactical usages that were more closely in accord with those of the Classical age. That is not to say that there are no non-Classical elements in Erasmus. As D. Thomson has pointed out in his chapter on Erasmus' style (Ch. V), Erasmus used a number of post-Classical words and idioms, but he did so with discrimination, when the context made it appropriate. But the foundation-stone of his whole style was a thorough knowledge of the Classical authors.

It is interesting to draw a comparison between the development of Latin style from the Carolingian revival to the time of Erasmus and its development from the earliest period to the Golden Age. In each case the earlier writers relied to a very great extent on literary devices based solely on the sound of words, in particular, assonance and alliteration, a technique to which the language is particularly well suited. In both cases the writers of a later age developed new methods that were more subtle and more sophisticated, as men began to write Latin more and more under the influence of Greek models. It was this interaction of Greek and Latin that brought about both the Golden Age of the Classical period and the new Classicism of Erasmus.

The letters of Erasmus have already been discussed in some detail by J. Binns (Ch. III). It is only necessary to add that in this *genre*, too, Erasmus goes back to the Classical period. Most of the collections of letters in the early Middle Ages had been official or pastoral. It was only with John of Salisbury, in the second half of the twelfth century, that we come across an interchange of letters on literary and intellectual subjects between members of a group possessing common interests. It is because the letters of Erasmus contain so much narrative and anecdotal material, so much of personal trivialities, so much that is light-hearted, that they bear so close a resemblance to the Ciceronian collection.

It remains to discuss depiction of character. In the earlier period the influence of Suetonius had been particularly strong. Einhard's portrayal of Charlemagne has already been mentioned, but William of Malmesbury followed the Suetonian technique closely, not merely in his formal biographies, such as the *Life of Wulfstan*,[1] but also in the biographical sketches he included in his histories, particularly his depiction of William Rufus and Henry I in the *Gesta Regum*. But William was more than a mere imitator of Suetonius. He had something that few, if any, Classical writers had, a keen interest in the development of character, and can give a convincing account of how a man's character changes as he goes through life. He is very successful in his description of the changes of character undergone by William Rufus and Roger, Bishop of Salisbury, the result, in the one case, of the removal of Lanfranc's wholesome influence and, in the other, of unbroken and excessive prosperity.

Other writers of this period produced character-sketches, usually in the form of obituaries, that consisted of a bare list of laudatory epithets. This technique was used by William of Jumièges and Orderic Vitalis. A typical example is Orderic's brief note on Edward the Confessor.

> Edwardus nempe rex vir bonus erat et humilis, mitis, iocundus et longanimis, amator Dei fidelis, et sanctae Ecclesiae defensor invincibilis, clemens pauperum tutor, et Anglicarum legum legitimus restitutor. (*Interpolations in William of Jumièges* VII. 9.)

> Indeed Edward was a good man and humble, gentle, cheerful and patient, a faithful lover of God and an invincible defender of the holy Church, a merciful guardian of the poor, and a lawful restorer of the laws of England.

It is interesting to note that even this short, straightforward sketch contains a certain amount of deliberate assonance and rhyme.

Henry of Huntingdon, in his character sketches, produced studied literary portraits. Sometimes there is a series of carefully chosen and often contrasting epithets, as with his brief sketch of Kinric of Wessex:

> Armorumque decus debellatorque ferarum, aetate tener sed armis acer, annis parvus sed vigore magnus. (IV. 18.)

> Glory of war and tamer of wild beasts, tender in age but fierce in arms, small in years but mighty in strength.

Or of Robert Bloet, Bishop of Lincoln:

Quo non erat alter forma venustior, mente serenior, affatu dulcior.
(VII. 3.)

Than whom there was no man more handsome in outward form,
more serene in spirit, more pleasant in speech.

Or of Remigius, his predecessor:

Erat siquidem statura parvus sed corde magnus, colore fuscus sed
operibus venustus. (VI. 41.)

He was small in stature but mighty in heart, dark in complexion
but fair in all his works.

Or of Ranulf Flambard:

Placitatori sed perversori, exactori sed exustori totius Angliae.
(VII. 21.)

The play on words cannot be rendered in English.

This element of contrast and antithesis comes out very strongly
in his character-sketch of Henry I (VIII. 1) where three good
qualities attributed to him—his wisdom, success in war and wealth
—are counterbalanced by three vices—avarice, cruelty, and lust.
This grouping in threes had already been used in his picture of
Canute, where he notes the Danish king's three great and glorious
exploits; the marriage of his daughter to the Emperor, his pilgrimage to Rome, and the incident of the tide (VI. 17). But his
most interesting character-sketch is that of William the Conqueror
(VI. 39). It is based on the Anglo-Saxon Chronicles, but the words
have been skilfully selected and arranged so as to make the greatest
possible use of the various literary devices such as rhyme, antithesis, oxymoron, and alliteration, the clauses being set out in
balanced groups of threes and fours.

Aelred of Rievaulx follows a similar technique in a number of
his character sketches, though he often varies the lists of epithets
by the use of chiasmus, as in his description of Prince Henry of
Scotland:

Erat autem adolescens pulchra facie et decorus aspectu, tantae
humilitatis ut omnibus inferior videretur, tantae auctoritatis ut ab
omnibus timeretur, tam dulcis, tam amabilis, tam affabilis ut di-
ligeretur ab omnibus; tam castus corpore, in sermone tam sobrius,
in cunctis moribus tam honestus, tam assiduus in ecclesia, orationi
tam intentus, tam benivolus circa pauperes, contra malefactores
tam erectus, sacerdotibus et monachis sic prostratus, ut et in rege
monachum et in monacho regem praetendere videretur. (*Relatio de
Standardo*, f. 198.)

He was a young man of handsome features and goodly to look upon, of such great humility that he seemed inferior to all men, of such great authority that he was feared by all men, so pleasant, affectionate, and friendly that he was loved by all men; so pure in body, so sober in speech, in all his behaviour so virtuous, so diligent in church, so devout in prayer, so kindly towards the poor, against evil-doers so upright, towards priests and monks so self-abasing, that he seemed to display the character of a monk in a king and a king in a monk.

The portrait of Henry's opponent, Walter Espec, bears some traces of Suetonian influence in the account of his physical appearance:

Vir senex et plenus dierum, acer ingenio, in consiliis prudens, in pace modestus, in bello providus, amicitiam sociis, fidem semper regibus servans. Erat ei statura ingens, membra omnia tantae magnitudinis ut nec modum excederent et tantae proceritati congruerent. Capilli nigri, barba prolixa, frons patens et libera, oculi grandes et perspicaces, facies amplissima, tracticia tamen, vox tubae similis; facundiam, quae ei facilis erat, quadam maiestate soni componens. Erat praeterea nobilis carne, sed Christiana pietate longe nobilior. (*Relatio de Standardo*, f. 196b.)

He was an old man and full of days, keen of wit, wise in counsel, modest in peace, far-sighted in war, a man who remained loyal to his friends and faithful always to his king. He was of vast stature, with all his limbs of such a size that they were not out of proportion but fitted his great height. He had black hair, a flowing beard, eyes big and piercing, features broad but wrinkled, and a voice like a trumpet; his oratory, which came readily to him, he delivered with a voice of majestic ring. He was, too, of noble blood, but far more noble in his Christian piety.

The last sentence contains a clear echo of Henry of Huntingdon's description of Archbishop Mellitus, 'Carne nobilis, sed mente nobilior,' (III. 22).

Aelred's description of King David of Scotland (*Genealogia*) is cast in a rather different form. The style is more Ciceronian, with frequent use of anaphora. The detailed account of David's last hours recalls the early medieval accounts of the deaths of saints. But there is a definite attempt to present a real picture of a man whom the writer knew and loved. In this respect it follows in the tradition of Eadmer's Life of Anselm, and points forward to Erasmus' portraits of Vitrarius, More and Colet.

As P. G. Bretenholz has pointed out,[2] Erasmus' account of the lives and characters of Vitrarius and Colet, contained in his letter to Jodocus Jonas,[3] is composed on the lines of a pair of Plutarch's *Parallel Lives*, ending as it does with an assessment of their comparative achievements. It is Plutarchan, too, in that the purpose of the exposition is to set out virtuous behaviour for imitation:

> Egregium aliquod pietatis exemplar, ad quod tuum institutum attemperes.

> An outstanding pattern of piety, to which you can adapt your own way of life.

The emphasis on the moral character of the subject is also Plutarchan, and as Mrs M. M. Phillips has pointed out in Chapter I of this volume, Plutarch was an author whom Erasmus held in high esteem. The depiction of Vitrarius begins with an account of his physical appearance and his character, and then goes on to his dislike of monastic life as being opposed to true Christianity, his devotion to St Paul, his methods of preaching, his selflessness, the merit of his disciples, his opposition to pointless ceremony and ritual, and his attack on the corruption associated with the Jubilee. It ends with a description of the attempt to excommunicate him, his successful defence, his demotion and explusion by his fellow-monks, and his death. The picture of Colet follows, *mutatis mutandis*, a very similar pattern. It starts with an account of his birth, family, and physical appearance, which is described in almost the same words as Erasmus has used for Vitrarius: 'Corpus elegans ac procerum (corpore procero et eleganti).'

Then Erasmus tells of his education, and, as with Vitrarius, describes his method of preaching. Then there is an account of his sober luncheon-parties and his simple dress. An account of the founding of St Paul's School leads on to the statement of Colet's conviction that the correct education of the young was of supreme importance to society. Erasmus next mentions his death, and after this more or less chronological account of Colet's career he proceeds to make a brief mention of three points, first, Colet's character, and how he successfully fought against his natural inclination towards pride, laziness, and love of money; then his unorthodox religious views, including his hatred of the hypocrisy of monastic life and the corruption of certain bishops—it is interesting to note that his views on confession are expressed in almost identical language to those of Vitrarius; and finally, to balance Vitrarius' troubles with his superiors, Colet's own danger of incurring the king's displeasure because of his criticism of Henry's war with France.

When we compare these two character-sketches with most of those of the twelfth century, what strikes our attention most of all is that with Erasmus the words are subordinated to the ideas. The literary devices employed, such as the pun *'gemmeum Vitrarium'*, the biting wit: 'Cui nemo prudens cauletum suum vellet committere' ('whom no man of any sense would put in charge of his cabbage-patch')—used of Vitrarius' successor as Warden of his monastery —and the striking phrases: 'Tota illius vita nihil erat nisi sacra contio' ('His whole life was a preaching of the Word of God'), all depended on the meaning of the words employed and not their sound.

These two character-sketches, when compared with their medieval counterparts, have a modernity about them. They represent an attempt to portray the real essence of a man's character and personality, instead of putting forward an artificial literary portrait in conventional terms. This modernity in so much of what Erasmus wrote underlines the truth of the saying that in many respects there is a closer link between the classical age and our own times than between either and the Middle Ages. Although critical techniques were in their infancy, Erasmus belonged to an age when men realized the need to apply intellectual criticism to inherited dogma. The supernatural and the miraculous elements that so many twelfth-century writers included in their works for the edification—or delectation—of their readers find no place in Erasmus. The fact that Erasmus wrote exclusively in Latin should not prevent us placing him in the modern rather than in the medieval world. When Erasmus was alive gunpowder had long been invented, printing displaced the copying of manuscripts, the Reformation came into being and—though it made but a slight ripple on the world's consciousness—America was discovered.

In many ways the attitudes of Erasmus towards contemporary problems are ones that we can view with sympathy. His outspoken condemnation of war, on the grounds that no dispute can be so serious as to justify warfare, with all its horrors, between Christian (i.e., civilized) peoples, is one that prevails today. So, too, was his belief that true Christianity consists in following a Christlike life rather than adherence to dogma or observance of ritual. His views on education were advanced and humane, and more congenial to our present educational outlook than were many of the ideas of

Victorian England. But it is his position in the great religious controversies of his times that is most significant to us now, though the bitter controversies of our contemporary world arise out of race rather than religion. The experiences of Erasmus are a warning to us that the man of moderate views, the genuine reformer, is always in danger of finding himself outflanked by the extremists, and often ends up by coming under the same fire as the very institutions that he had taken the lead in attacking. This is often the fate of the opponent of violence, the man whose aim it is to change rather than to destroy. It is what happens now to many of those who take the same attitudes as Erasmus did towards the important issues of the day.

Erasmus was the last great Latin writer. Already the vernacular literatures in the various countries of Europe had produced works of great merit, with Chaucer in England and Dante and Petrarch in Italy, and the Reformation encouraged linguistic as well as religious nationalism. In the next important literary era in England, the Elizabethan age, some Latin works of literature of considerable merit were produced—the plays of William Gager, for example[4]—but the great names, Spenser, Shakespeare, and Marlowe, wrote in English, as did Thomas More's successor in the field of political philosophy, Francis Bacon.

In Erasmus, people today can find someone who wrote a style of Latin that was, for the most part, simple, lucid and elegant, someone who, as regards fundamentals, belonged to our own era, or at any rate to the era to which our parents belonged. Erasmus was in close touch with the leading figures of the Reformation, including Luther; he was an intimate friend of men such as More and Colet, Fisher and Warham, who did so much to bring about the educational revival that took place in England at that time; he corresponded with the most notable scholars and writers in Europe, men like Reuchlin, Rhenanus and von Hutten. As a result, much of what he wrote is of unparalleled value as first-hand evidence for the political, religious and social history of the times. He played a leading part in the development of publishing, working first with Aldus and then with Froben. On top of all this, he was one of the greatest masters of Latin that there has ever been. In his hands Latin became, once again, a truly living language, that can be read by students of our own times without too much difficulty and with great enjoyment.

NOTES

[1] *Cf.* D. H. Farmer, 'Two Biographies of William of Malmesbury', in *Latin Biography*, ed. T. A. Dorey, Routledge & Kegan Paul, 1967.

[2] P. G. Bretenholz, *History and Biography in the Work of Erasmus of Rotterdam*, Geneva, 1966.

[3] Allen, *Erasmi Epistolae*, IV. 507–27 (1211).

[4] Recent editions of Gager's works include: Allison Leon (ed.), *Meleager*, Birmingham University Press, 1968; Pauline Cairns (ed.), *Ulysses Redux*, Birmingham University Press; J. W. Binns (ed.), *Manuscript Poems*, Birmingham University Press, 1965.

ERASMUS

Index of Names

Adrian VI, Pope, 65
Aelred of Rievaulx, 140, 147,
    148, 152, 153
Agricola, Rudolph, 3, 16
Aldus Manutius, 6, 7, 19, 21,
    90, 95, 156
Aleandro, 86, 88, 104
Ammonius, Andrew, 63
Amorbach, 87, 92
Apuleius, 25, 124
Aquinas, Thomas, 90, 100
Aristophanes, 6, 19, 20
Aristotle, 6, 17, 19, 20, 91
Athenaeus, 19, 21
Augustine, St, 59, 65, 71, 83,
    84, 88, 135, 139
Ausonius, 139

Bade, Josh (Badius), 7, 87, 123
Basil, St, 59, 116
Bath, Bishop of, 140, 144
Batt, James, 25, 68, 84, 90
Becket, Thomas, 108, 130, 140
Bede, 139, 143
Bilney, Thomas, 98, 99
Blount, Charles, 17, 18
Boccaccio, 19, 131
Boner, 11, 17
Budaeus, William (Budé), 64,
    90, 92, 96, 116, 117, 123, 127,
    129

Caesar, Julius, 19, 122, 140, 149
Calvin, John, 107, 111
Cambrai, Bishop of, 58, 86
Canossa, Cardinal, 130
Cassiodorus, 123, 124
Cato, 6, 7, 129, 139
Charlemagne, 139, 149, 151
Charles V, 58, 107, 108
Chrysostom, 66, 68
Cicero, 3, 5, 6, 7, 12, 13, 14,
    19, 20, 21, 24, 25, 28, 43, 55,
    59, 60, 61, 75, 109, 115, 118,
    119, 120, 122, 123, 124, 125,
    127, 131, 132, 133, 134, 139,
    140, 143, 148, 149
Claudian, 3, 139
Colet, John, 4, 63, 86, 89, 90,
    91, 95, 106, 108, 117, 118,
    121, 130, 153, 154, 156
Columella, 20
Curtius, Q., 6
Cyprian, 59, 71

Demosthenes, 6, 17, 18
Diogenes Laertius, 19
Du Bellay, 25
Duns Scotus, 28, 88, 127

Eadmer, 140, 141, 143, 153
Einhard, 139, 151